CHRISTIAN AND MORAL ACTION

The Institute for the Psychological Sciences Monograph Series

GENERAL EDITOR: *Craig Steven Titus*

The Institute for the Psychological Sciences (IPS) Monograph Series publishes original scholarly works that promote studies in the broad field of the psychological sciences. The Institute espouses the view that interdisciplinary conversations among experts in psychology, philosophy, and religion serve to advance our understanding of what constitutes both the mental well-being and the spiritual flourishing of the human person.

The overall mission of IPS is to contribute to the renewal of the Catholic Christian intellectual tradition and to the integration of the theoretical and practical bases of the science of psychology and a Catholic view of the person. IPS remains committed at the same time to fruitful dialogue with voices from outside of the Christian tradition. The Institute offers a Master of Science and Psy.D. degrees in Clinical Psychology and a Master of Science in General Psychology. Moreover, it initiates research projects through the Scholarly Research Center located in Arlington, Virginia.

The IPS Monograph Series is placed under the patronage of St. Albert the Great, a thirteenth-century man of science and faith, whose life incarnates the human values that the Institute for the Psychological Sciences aims to promote. Those scholars associated with IPS seek to maintain a constructive and critical conversation based on both advanced research about and a high vision of the human person. IPS is committed to integrating what is the best in faith-based traditions and what is judged worthwhile in the several life sciences.

*The Institute for the Psychological Sciences
Monograph Series*

VOLUME 3

CHRISTIAN AND MORAL ACTION

Kevin L. Flannery, SJ

The Institute for the Psychological Sciences Press
Arlington, Virginia

Nihil Obstat: Rev. Francisco J. Egnaña, SJ
Censor Deputatus
Imprimatur: † Paul S. Loverde
Bishop of Arlington
June 8, 2012

The *Nihil Obstat* and *Imprimatur* are official declarations that a book or pamphlet is free of doctrinal or moral error. No implication is contained therein that those who have granted the *Nihil Obstat* and *Imprimatur* agree with the contents, opinions, or statements expressed.

Distributed by:
The Catholic University of America Press
620 Michigan Ave. N.E. /240 Leahy Hall
Washington, DC 20064

The paper used in this publication meets the minimum requirements of American National Standards for Information Sciences— Permanence of Paper for Printed Library Materials, ANSI z39.48-1984

Cataloging-in-Publication Data available from the Library of Congress

For Ralph McInerny

CONTENTS

INTRODUCTION

Ralph McInerny said of Étienne Gilson that he was "a wise man whose late works are aimed generally at the intelligent, not the learned."[1] Without making claims to his stature as a wise man, my aim in this small book is not unlike the later Gilson's. As I wrote it, I had in mind not my colleagues in the philosophical/theological sector of academia (we, presumably, being "learned" in the matters treated here), but the intelligent, well-educated reader whose formal education is not necessarily in philosophy or theology. The only thing I would add to the Gilsonian aim is that I conceive of this reader as not having at his disposal, when he takes up this book, a large stretch of time available for study. This reader is not disinclined, however, to engage in careful reflection. The argumentation of the book is straightforward and the terminology nontechnical, but it does require close attention.

Five of the seven chapters of this book were originally commissioned by Ralph McInerny for the online International Catholic University.[2] The sixth and seventh were added later, upon the suggestion of Craig Steven Titus. The first five were written as spoken lectures, although this was always a bit of a fiction, since they were never intended to be delivered individually as lectures. (I did, however, deliver an amalgamation of three of them in a television stu-

---

1. Ralph McInerny, *Some Catholic Writers* (South Bend, Ind.: St. Augustine's Press, 2007), 63.

2. To date, the chapters have not appeared on that website; if and when they do, they will do so under a password.

dio in South Bend, Indiana, before an amused audience consisting of Ralph, Dan Osberger, and various technicians.) The spoken lecture fiction is suited also to this print medium, for it allows me to speak not infrequently in the first person. The point of doing this is not to be chummy, but to make it apparent that often what I say is not to be considered doctrine, nor even to represent the consensus of Catholic scholars, but is rather my own opinion.

My very special thanks are due to Elizabeth Kirk, who took a personal interest in the book, providing many useful comments and posing several difficult questions that served to improve the book considerably. I would also like to thank for their helpful comments Fr. Stephen Brock, Ralph McInerny, John Finnis (especially for comments on the final paragraphs of chapter 5), Janet Smith, Helen Watt, Peter Furlong, and Fr. McLean Cummings. I wrote chapters 1 through 5 while holding the Remick Senior Visiting Fellowship at the Center for Ethics and Culture at the University of Notre Dame. I am immensely grateful to the Center, and especially to David Solomon, for granting me this fellowship and for providing me with an extremely pleasant context within which to work. Chapter 5 was delivered as an address on March 10, 2010, as part of a conference in Rome on medical ethics organized by the Center for Ethics and Culture. It was then published in *Christian Bioethics* 17 (2011) and appears here with permission. I thank several of those present at the conference, especially David Solomon, Bryan Pilkington, and Jeffrey Bishop, for forcing me to clarify some issues. Finally, although these chapters were not part of my (occasional) activities at the Institute for the Psychological Sciences in Arlington, Virginia, the Institute has been supportive of them as long as it has known of them. For this I thank Romanus Cessario, Gladys Sweeney, and Craig Steven Titus.

I have written a number of things on topics discussed in this small book. A list of these publications (and others) can be found under my name at the website of the Pontifical Gregorian University (http://www.unigre.it/).

CHRISTIAN AND MORAL ACTION

one

IS MORAL TEACHING THE CHURCH'S?

The first point of business in any intellectual enterprise is to establish the nature and the proper understanding of what one intends to talk about, for, if the subject matter is itself not intelligible, the enterprise harbors the cause of its own eventual disintegration at its very core. We are presented here in this first chapter with a number of questions: Is there such a thing as *the church's* moral teaching, as opposed to moral teaching simply speaking? If so, what is the relationship between this teaching and morality itself? Can a precept contained in the church's teaching be imposed upon a person who does not recognize the church's authority?

The best way to approach such questions is, I believe, by way of a four-part distinction found near the beginning of Thomas Aquinas's so-called "treatise on law" [*Summa Theologiae, (ST)* 1-2.90–108]. Drawing on St. Augustine, Aquinas says that there are four types of law: eternal, natural, human, and divine.

To call the first of these "law" seems strange, especially once one realizes that it—that is, eternal law—is not distinct from God himself [*ST* 1-2.91.1 ad 3]. But this becomes more understandable if one bears in mind that at the heart of the concept of law are reason and order. There is nothing in the universe more reasonable or more orderly than God himself, so that, as a person or a society grows closer to God, he or it becomes more reasonable and orderly, more peaceful and dependable.

The second type of law, natural law, is not unconnected with eternal law. It is basically the ordering of nature *toward* eternal law: toward God. This relationship is sometimes referred to as natural law's participation in eternal law. Within nature we find, of course, man, who has a nature of his own. Man's nature comes from above; each of God's creatures comes into being, lives, and even dies, in the particular way designed for it by eternal law. In man natural law becomes manifest especially in his natural inclinations, such as his inclination to remain in existence, his inclination to reproduce, and his inclination to know God and to live in a rational manner in human society [*ST* 1-2.94.2].

Since we are speaking about man in general, and not about what any individual man would do, when we speak of living in a rational manner we must take into consideration the characteristic ways in which *man* orders society. Obviously not everything man does in ordering society is done well, just as not everything he does when following his inclination to survive or to reproduce is done well, but the types of things he does in society are important for understanding natural law as it applies to man. Men characteristically do things that other animals do not. Men build places of worship, for instance, and they marry. Just as it belongs to the nature of bees to build honeycombs or to the nature of birds to protect their young, it belongs to the nature of man to organize his society according to professions, sciences, and social roles (such as husband and wife). We shall see in these chapters that, in many situations, such natural human structures are decisive for determining what it is moral—or immoral—to do.

Like natural law, the third type of law, human law, looks toward eternal law, but is more removed from it. Natural law concerns what man does by nature; human law concerns the particular ways he decides to put into effect the things determined by natural law (and therefore ultimately by eternal law). As such, human law is more variable than natural law. An example will be useful. Part of natural law is the precept that we ought to take measures to avoid harming others; human law carries through on this precept by instituting traffic laws. Traffic laws differ from society to society—some permit driving on the right, some driving on the left. This variety is in no way a violation of natural law; in fact, in many such matters, it would be unnatural to insist on uniformity.

The fourth type of law, divine law, despite its name, is distinct from eternal law—not least because it is not God. But it is also distinct from natural and human law insofar as it is information that comes from God through or in his spokesmen. Divine law includes all the precepts pertaining to Christian living that are contained in divine revelation. God has revealed moral precepts to men naturally. This is obvious from the many people who have had no contact with either the Jewish or Christian religions, but who have nonetheless correctly understood at least some parts of natural law. A good example would be Aristotle, whose moral theory was largely taken over by Thomas Aquinas, but who knew nothing of revelation. But God has also revealed moral precepts in a supernatural way by speaking to us through the authors of Old and New Testament writings and especially by speaking in Jesus Christ his Son. This direct information, insofar as it bears upon the way we live our lives, is divine law.

It is important to make these distinctions among the various types of law and to understand their interrelationships in order to head off some very common arguments against Christian efforts to influence the shape of civil society: efforts to protect the institution of marriage, for instance, or to place limits (and ultimately a ban) upon the killing of unborn children. One such argument is sometimes heard even in the mouths of Christian politicians and pundits: "Personally and by religious conviction," the argument often goes, "I am opposed to such practices, but I cannot impose my views on others." That would be acceptable if the basis of the argument against such practices were divine law: law binding for Christians *as* Christians, for instance, or for Catholics *as* Catholics. But in fact the church has always understood that such issues as abortion fall not under divine, but under natural law, which is binding on all men by virtue of what they are. So, the conversation in the public square takes as its binding principles the principles of natural law. It is into this conversation, and not into any conversation about divine law, that the truly Christian politician or pundit wishes to enter—and has every right to enter.

So, does this mean that in the field of morality divine and eternal law have no role, that they are unnecessary? Let us begin with eternal law. Eternal law is both necessary and unnecessary. As we have seen, it is not distinct from God himself, so, it is necessary if there is to be any morality at all, since nature and its ordering come from God and could come from no other source. But a belief in the existence of eternal law—in the existence of God—is not necessary to give true and convincing reasons that people, whether they believe in God or not, ought to organize their lives in accordance with the precepts of natural law.

Imagine a civilization with factories and farms, but wholly contained within a single opaque sphere. Daytime and nighttime alternate as lamps high above shine and grow dim. You, a scientist, live in the sphere along with many other people, including another scientist. The type of science you both do concerns, to a large extent, light. As it happens, you have been outside of the sphere and know that the light comes into the sphere by way of a huge solar panel—and ultimately from the sun. Your friend, the other scientist, has never been outside and thinks you have imagined the outside, the solar panel, and the sun. He thinks that, with the lamps within the sphere, there is simply nothing more to explain: light comes from the lamps, and that's all there is to it. Still, despite such predispositions, he is a very careful scientist and understands the essential properties of light, as do you. It is perfectly possible for you to work together with the other scientist, given what he knows about light, none of which you dispute.

The church's engagement in the secular political conversation is something like that. It does not *need* to invoke God, and it knows that, in such a context, doing so would make its arguments and statements easier to dismiss. ("That is all very nice, your Excellency, but I am not a believer.") Relying simply upon what they know about the nature of man, including the way he organizes himself naturally, Christians can make claims about how society ought to be organized, what practices it ought to permit or prohibit, and so on. Of course, someone who does not want to hear what Christians say about how things should be can always challenge the premises Christians draw from natural law; such a person can also deny the existence of natural law. But he cannot exclude the arguments proposed simply on the grounds that they are put forward by people who believe in God and who believe that what they propose is in accordance with eternal law. These arguments, if they are well-constructed, will make use only of those truths knowable to those whose experience is limited to the natural: to those who have never, so to speak, left the sphere lit by the sun. The individual living Christian has never left the sphere of natural law, but he is one with a person who has: Jesus Christ.

What then about divine law? Given that all we need in order to participate in political life is natural law, is not divine law's status greatly reduced? And how can it be right that the merely natural is placed above the supernatural? The answer here is simply that, yes, in the political realm, considered *as* the political realm, divine law is of limited use. But in the life of the individual Christian, who may very well be engaged in government or the legal profession, divine law is enormously important, since by means of it he knows that certain ways of organizing society cannot be correct. He knows, for example, that no matter what the arguments, it is never moral directly to kill a human being. So, although he may have to argue for this position with someone who rejects divine law, he has no real need of such argumentation for his own sake: on perfectly rational grounds, he can—indeed, he ought—to accept the position because of the authority of the church, which passes on, interprets, and applies the truths of revelation also as they pertain to the moral sphere.

In the 1970s some theologians argued that the church does not have the authority to teach in a binding way regarding particular human acts. They argued that, although it can put forward teachings regarding practices described generally, it is not competent to teach that all actions of a particular type—all abortions, for example, or all lies—are immoral. Sometimes the argument ran in this fashion: when the church makes reference in a teaching to a certain type of action—murder, for instance, or lying—saying that it is immoral, it is making reference to acts that need to be picked out from a larger class of acts *as* the immoral ones. Thus, murder refers to *bad* killings, lying to *bad* acts of telling a falsehood with the intention to deceive. We must (it was argued) interpret the church's teaching about adultery, contraception, masturbation, etc., in a similar manner—that is, as not yet speaking about particular acts, but just about general concepts.

The point made by these theologians was not that, before judging a particular action done by a person, one has to determine whether he knew what he was doing and did what he did freely—for that such factors limit culpability is admitted by all—but rather that no one (the church included) can determine the moral character of a particular action before considering all the other circumstances pertaining to it. Thus, although the church might say that, for instance, contraception is wrong, the final determination of the morality of a particular act of contraception can only be made by the person acting, as he considers all the circumstances. For these theologians this consideration of the circumstances often involved an estimation of the "proportion of good" to be achieved by not following the norm in question; their approach became known as proportionalism. In his encyclical letter *Veritatis splendor,* John Paul II rejected proportionalism as incompatible with the faith.

Even independently of *Veritatis splendor,* however, it is obvious that the dissenting approach just described is incompatible with the historical practice of the church, which has never given any indication, when issuing prohibitions regarding types of moral acts, that it does not mean all the acts falling under that particular description, whether or not it might seem to the person acting—or to a theologian—that a particular act would bring about positive results. Thus, when the church teaches, for instance, that adultery is wrong, it means that any act of sexual intercourse with someone not one's spouse or with the spouse of another is immoral (provided that the person knows who is married and whose spouse is whose [!] and that he acts freely), even if, for instance, the spouse of the other is long since civilly divorced and in desperate need of intimate companionship. If one does not assume this, it is impossible to make sense of the history of canon law regarding marriage (which allows marriage only if a previous "marriage" never existed or an actual marriage no longer exists). In teaching in this manner, the church is carrying on the ministry of the Son of God, who reprimanded his fellow Jews for their hardness of heart regarding marriage and divorce.

A number of times since the 1970s, the church has effectively repudiated claims by theologians that the church is not competent to issue teachings in a binding manner regarding particular types of acts. In his 1995 encyclical letter *Evangelium vitae,* John Paul II issued a highly authoritative pronouncement regarding abortion. It reads as follows:

> Therefore, by the authority that Christ conferred upon Peter and his Successors, in communion with the Bishops—who on various occasions have condemned abortion and who in the aforementioned consultation, albeit dispersed throughout the world, have shown unanimous agreement concerning this doctrine—I declare that direct abortion, that is, abortion willed as an end or as a means, always constitutes a grave moral disorder, since it is the deliberate killing of an innocent human being [§62].

He goes on to say that this teaching is based upon natural law and upon divine revelation. And then he adds: "No circumstance, no purpose, no law whatsoever can ever make licit an act which is intrinsically illicit, since it is contrary to the Law of God which is written in every human heart, knowable by reason itself, and proclaimed by the Church" [§62]. For one who accepts that the church is a source of divine law, there can be little doubt that no particular act of the sort identified can be moral. In the same document (at §65), John Paul II makes a similar declaration regarding euthanasia.

Before concluding this chapter, I must make a final, related point. It pertains to a larger issue—the responsibilities of public officials and personalities with respect to church teaching. The point is this: that, although the church can issue teachings concerning particular acts, some of its moral teachings do indeed remain at a general level. These teachings pertain especially to policy decisions made at an official level in civil government—with regard, for instance, to the relief of poverty, the control of immigration, the initiation of war, or the punishment of crime. The church can and does issue teachings regarding such matters and often does so in such a way that it is crystal clear what it thinks should be done in a particular instance; and yet it can remain true, and this is acknowledged by the church, that the actual policy decisions belong properly to the authorities in charge, who have access to the relevant facts and have also greater knowledge of—and experience in—the political sphere. This is all part of the recognition that there are within the church many genuine callings—many genuine vocations—each with its characteristic principles and responsibilities.[1]

The possibility that there might be a legitimate difference of prudential judgment between the church's teaching magisterium and the person or persons responsible for making political decisions depends, in the first place, upon the type of policy at issue. If the church says to a regime that it ought to discontinue a program of genocide, even though that teaching is about policy, it does not presume that a head of state could possibly continue with the genocide and still be acting

1. See *Lumen gentium* §§30–42.

morally. The same cannot be said, however, of a declaration of war, provided the war is not clearly an unjust one. In its motherly care for all its children, the church must always be the promoter of peace; war, as John Paul II never tired of saying, is always a sign of human failure. And yet it is not the church's role to decide, for example, when threats or incursions from a neighboring state have become too frequent or worrisome to be ignored. That is the role of those entrusted with the common good of the state concerned.

This is not to say, however, that, as long as the proposed policy involves no intrinsic evil such as that of genocide, the person with civil authority enjoys complete independence of ethical judgment. There are many things we do that are wrong, but not in the indubitable way that genocide or abortion are wrong: eating or drinking too much, for example, or chastising a child too harshly or too often; and the same goes for policies enacted by political entities. In all such questions both the church and public officials are obliged to follow the promptings of the natural law—which, as St. Paul says, speaks in the heart of all men [Rom. 2.14–15]. If, for instance, the prolonged presence of a nation's army on foreign soil begins to tip the balance toward injustice, it does so insofar as it is against natural law. When the head of state of this nation, face to face with the pertinent information, sees—we might even say, *feels*—that the balance has been so tipped, he acts morally in rectifying matters appropriately.

two

THE INTELLIGIBILITY OF
HUMAN ACTION

In chapter 1 we discussed primarily how natural law relates to eternal law and to divine law; our task in this second chapter is to discuss how human actions relate to natural law.[1] This is basically to consider morality, since morality is about whether human actions and the dispositions they yield correspond to natural law. Of course, morality also looks to human law. With certain exceptions, such as a law ordering one to perform an abortion, we are morally obliged to follow the laws of the society in which we live. But the reason we are obliged to follow the laws of society (human law) is that not so doing is against natural law. The actions and laws of a perfect human society would be consistent with natural and eternal law.

In this chapter and later ones, I shall be using a term that requires some explanation: "intelligible." It is Aristotelian in origin. Anything that belongs to the intellectual order is obviously intelligible: ideas,

---

1. A human action is an action for which a person is morally responsible; in what follows, for the sake of brevity, I occasionally refer to human actions simply as actions.

arguments, syllogisms are all intelligible entities. They are such because we can understand them. But sometimes intelligible entities are joined together in such a way that, as joined together, they are not intelligible. For example, the terms "beer," "odd," and "parse" are all intelligible in themselves; when, however, they are strung together as "beer parse odd," they are unintelligible. Some things existing outside the human mind are also intelligible: "what it is to be a rabbit" would be an example, since there is a certain logic to a rabbit's nature that holds any rabbit together as a rabbit. Natural human practices are also intelligible: marriage, for instance, is intelligible, since, when it is entered into fully and according to its nature, it makes sense. A couple may have trouble *in* their marriage, but marriage itself, since it is part of man's nature, cannot turn out to be incoherent—any more than a rabbit's nature can itself turn out to be incoherent. God is also intelligible, in the sense that we can understand things about him, although his full intelligibility is beyond our comprehension.

An organization can be broken down into its various parts in order to understand and assess its intelligibility—in order to understand, that is, how well the parts fit together and function within the whole. An army, for instance, can be broken down into component parts such as its officers, its enlisted men, weapons, and food supplies in order to see how it works and whether the parts are functioning well together. Some component parts can themselves be broken down. To understand a rifle, for instance, a soldier is taught to break it down into its component parts and then to reverse the process so that, in the end, he grasps its intelligibility: how it functions. If there is a flaw in the rifle preventing its smooth functioning, that is bad for the rifle and for the army. Also, if there is some aspect of the rifle that makes it unsuitable for use within the army, that too is bad—even if it does not impair the functioning of the rifle as a rifle.

Morality can be understood in a similar way. Its intelligibility is more complicated and more nuanced than that of an army, but, like an army, the standard of goodness is intelligibility: to be bad is to lack functional intelligibility in some way. In this chapter we shall be concerned primarily, but not solely, with the analysis of human actions. If in the analysis—the breakdown—of a human action we find, for example, some flaw that vitiates its internal order or some part that does not fit into a larger segment of the whole, that is not good, because a lack of intelligibility indicates a failure to belong to—or be consistent with—natural law.

Human actions are intelligible entities: they are essentially ideas or thoughts directed in a particular way, although they are usually *about* concrete things—i.e., things that are not just ideas or thoughts. Since human actions are intelligible in this way, their moral analysis is a tricky business. Their parts are not as stable as are, for instance, the parts of a rifle. As the soldier is learning his rifle, he can go back to it time and time again; its parts will be the same as they were previously, and they will fit together in the same way. Human actions, on the other hand, are ephemeral and endlessly variable. In seeking to understand human actions, one can use standard examples that, in their abstract way, have a sort of stability, but actions themselves do not sit still in this way. Once an action is performed, it is gone—and it can never be an exact copy of any other action.

But, although actions are by nature extremely fluid and changeable, there are a number of factors that channel and shape them; by considering these, we can analyze actions in a satisfactory manner. The two main limiting factors are ignorance and force—which is only to say that one cannot do something in the moral sense unless one understands what one is doing and is not forced to do it. These two limiting factors have a direct bearing upon what are traditionally called the "sources of morality": the intention of an action, its circumstances, and its object. Intentions, objects, and (at least) some circumstances enter into the structure of actions, so they are among the parts of the mechanism we are here disassembling or analyzing in order to understand them. They are intelligible, although they can be parts of structures that are not intelligible—that is to say, they can be parts of evil acts—just as words that are intelligible in themselves can be put into sentences that are not themselves intelligible.

Let us examine the sources of morality—intention, circumstances, and object—in that order. The word "intention" comes from the Latin word *tendere,* meaning to tend toward [something or some state]; but, since we are now speaking from within the sphere of morality, we must understand this tending in a volitional way. Beer tends to grow flat once the bottle is opened, but we would not say that it has the intention to do so or that it does so intentionally. Another point is that intentions sometimes fall under other intentions. Consider an example used by Thomas Aquinas. A thief steals a golden cup (a chalice) from a temple, thereby committing the crime of sacrilege. The thief may very well have the intention of desecrating a temple: that would then be his overall intention. In order to accomplish this, he steals the cup. In order to do this he walks to the temple. And in order to do this he puts on shoes. All these things—the overall intention, stealing the cup, walking to the temple, putting on shoes—can be regarded as pertaining to a single action (an act of sacrilege), held together as one by the overall intention. But the subsidiary parts of this one action—walking, pulling on shoes—are also intended.

We might say that intention—or intentions—light up the physical actions that a person performs: the intention to desecrate the temple lights up all the actions involved in getting the cup, although each of those actions is presumably intentional in its own right. There can be no genuinely human act—nothing to consider morally—unless such light is present. This light is the light of the intellect, working together with the free will of the acting person. So, literally *everything* in morality—and, in particular, the moral character of the acts a person performs—depends on intention, which is a combination of both intellect and will.

Hearing for the first time that everything in morality depends on intention makes some people uncomfortable, since it seems to imply that, if someone (such as a judge or bishop) ever criticizes another for some act, that person can always reply that his *intention* was not to do *x*, but was rather to effect this or that good. But this should be no cause for uneasiness, since a person's intention is more knowing than any such facile reply would indicate. In other words, a person cannot choose what to include within the domain of his own intention, since intention is bound up with intellect and what intellect sees before it, it cannot *not* see. Consider again a man stealing a gold cup. It is true that, if the man does not realize that the building from which he is stealing the cup is a temple, he cannot commit sacrilege. But if he does know that the building is a temple and knows what sacrilege is, even if he has no interest in committing sacrilege, he does commit sacrilege, since all that information is in his intention—and his intellect—whether he likes it or not.

An attentive reader will have noticed a qualifying clause included in the former remark, which complicates matters a bit. The clause was this: "if he … knows what sacrilege is." Before going on to consider the object of the moral act, we must make a very brief excursus in order to address a worry possibly provoked by this clause. Let us say that a clever thief comes before the judge and says, "I do not *believe* that sacrilege is immoral, so obviously I do not *know* that it is immoral; you cannot, therefore, condemn me for committing sacrilege." In fact, the thief could make the same sort of argument about theft: "I do not believe that theft is immoral; therefore, I did not do anything immoral—since knowledge is necessary for an act to be judicable morally." The appropriate reaction to such an argument would be to invoke again the sovereignty of intellect. The accused man may not believe that sacrilege is immoral, but he knows what sacrilege is, so, whether he likes it or not, and whether he believes that committing sacrilege is moral or not, he has committed sacrilege (which, as a matter of fact, is an immoral thing to do).

The mistaken claim being made here by the thief and desecrator of the temple is basically a claim of conscience. I shall treat this theme more extensively in chapter 6, but it will be useful to make a few remarks about it here. Such claims of conscience are quite popular nowadays, even in certain sectors of the church (usually academic sectors). It is worth considering, therefore, what the *Catechism of the Catholic Church* has to say about conscience. Ignorance of the moral law, it says,

> can often be imputed to personal responsibility. This is the case when a man "takes little care to find out what is true and good, or when conscience is by degrees almost blinded through the habit of committing sin." In such cases, the person is culpable for the evil he commits.[2]

Note that such a person, ignorant because he does not want to hear about what he ought to do, is still "culpable for the evil he commits" in such a state. That is, he is culpable not only for not knowing the moral law or bearing it in mind, but also for any immoral acts that such ignorance leads him to commit. So, the knowledge that bears with it culpability can be very tenuous, indeed. It includes not just a thief's actually knowing that stealing a golden cup from a temple is sacrilege, but even his knowing there is reason to believe there is a law making stealing from a temple a special crime. In the realm of morals, even such attenuated knowledge is very potent: still very much beyond the power of the acting person to wish it away. We see this also in ignorance of things other than the law. If a man testing his rifle shoots into bushes within which it is reasonable to believe another person might be concealed, if he kills a person there concealed, he is held culpable for doing so, even though, strictly speaking (that is, in a strong sense), he did not know of anyone's presence there.

That brings us to the second source of morality, the object. In the sacrilege case, the object of the thief's act is the cup—or, describing the object more amply, the cup "*qua* stealable," i.e., as entering into that moral action. Once again, it is essential to bear in mind that the object of a moral act is something intelligible: it has its existence only

---

2. *Catechism of the Catholic Church* §1791 (quoting *Gaudium et spes* §16).

as falling under an intention—which, though primarily an act of the will, is also bound up with intellect. In *Veritatis splendor*, John Paul II writes as follows:

> The morality of the human act depends primarily and fundamentally on the "object" rationally chosen by the deliberate will, as is borne out by the insightful analysis, still valid today, made by Saint Thomas. In order to be able to grasp the object of an act which specifies that act morally, it is therefore necessary to place oneself in the perspective of the acting person.[3]

The pope's speaking here of placing oneself "in the perspective of the acting person" is a confirmation of what we have been saying thus far. If a flood should wash the golden cup that was in the temple into a man's house or if the cup were to be placed into his hands while he, unconscious, is carried by others into his house, he would not have committed theft or sacrilege or any such moral act, since a moral act is not a merely physical event, nor any event in which the agent's will and intellect are not involved.

As with intention, however, there is no dearth of those who misinterpret the pope in this regard, understanding him to be excluding *any* consideration of the physical from the analysis of moral acts. Thus, to use an example at the epicenter of the current debate, in determining whether it is moral for two spouses, one of whom has AIDS, to employ a prophylactic (a condom) in sexual intercourse, some theologians say that we must look to the intelligible reason for using the prophylactic (to prevent disease) and not to the physical characteristics of the act—i.e., to the fact that a barrier is placed between man and wife, preventing full marital union.

Fortunately, as we have just seen, in the same breath as his remark about the perspective of the acting person, John Paul II cites Thomas Aquinas on the object of the act, saying that his analysis is "still valid today." Thomas has no problem at all with the idea that physical char-

---

3. *Veritatis splendor* §78, citing Thomas Aquinas *ST* 1-2.18.6.

acteristics might enter into the moral analysis of acts. In a passage close by the one that the pope cites, Thomas considers the objection of someone who would argue that the moral character of an act cannot come from the object, since there is no evil in *things,* but only in the way that sinners use them. His answer is as follows:

> Although exterior things are in themselves good, still, they do not always have the due proportion to this or that action; and so, in as much as they are considered objects of such actions, they do not have the character of good.[4]

In other words, physical characteristics, although good insofar as they are created by God, can make actions bad. Exterior things do enter into the analysis of actions. They do so, we might add, whether the acting person wishes them to do so or not. To use the example before us, the use of a prophylactic by a couple does not have due proportion to the conjugal act. This lack of due proportion is a lack of intelligibility: not a complete lack of intelligibility, of course, since the couple presumably has a reason for using the prophylactic, but lack of fit between the use of that device and the conjugal act. The conjugal act is defined—not by man, but by nature—as complete physical union between a man and his wife; a prophylactic impedes this union. Obviously, the physical aspect of the conjugal act is not the only thing that enters into such analysis: the marital status of the parties involved and their awareness of what they are doing, for instance, are also important; but the physical is certainly not peripheral to the morality of what is done.

The third source of morality is circumstances. One more indication that natural law is not the private property of the church is that Thomas Aquinas takes his list of circumstances from the pagan Cicero, to which list he adds one circumstance from Aristotle (another pagan). According to Cicero, the (possibly) morally relevant circumstances include "who, what, where, by what means, why, how,

---

4. *ST* 1-2.18.2 ad 1.

and when"; the Aristotelian addition is "about what" [*ST* 1-2.7.3]. The word "circumstance" literally means to stand around something—that is, not to enter into the thing itself; and many circumstances do exactly that: they are associated with an action but do not enter into it morally. If I steal your car, it does not much matter whether I steal it from your driveway or from a parking lot downtown; in either case my crime is stealing. In my stealing your car, this circumstance ("where") has a status much like any incidental feature belonging to a substance, such as a man's height or the color of his hair. Such accidents are truly attributed to him (the substance), but they have little to do with what he is: a human being.

But because human actions are essentially intelligible things, and because what a circumstance may contribute to moral analysis is a way of understanding it—which is to say that a circumstance enters into moral analysis *as* an intelligible entity—circumstances can sometimes determine the very substance of what a person is doing. The situation is not like that of accidents with respect to a man's essence, where having red hair, for instance, is an entirely different sort of thing from being a man. Since both actions and circumstances are essentially intelligible entities (entities of reason), it is not impossible that a circumstance might become part and parcel of what someone is doing in performing an action. That is what we see in the sacrilege example. The thief steals the golden cup: that is the basic act he performs. (Its object, again, is the cup—or the cup "*qua* stealable.") But the cup happens to be in a temple. Being in a temple is a circumstance, the circumstance "where"; but in this case the circumstance transforms the thief's act from a mere act of theft into an act of sacrilege. Whether a circumstance does so transform an act depends on many factors, but the factors ultimately come down to whether or not an act in that circumstance is reasonable or intelligible (in the broader sense), given the justly formulated laws of the society in which it is performed.

That then concludes my consideration of the sources of morality (intention, object, and circumstances). Obviously, there is a great deal more to be said about how the sources of morality are identified and assessed, but the present context does not permit a more extensive treatment. There is, however, one issue that I cannot leave unaddressed, since it plays such an important part in natural law theory. Before introducing the three sources of morality, I mentioned that, although the material of morality, being intelligible, is very fluid, there are two main factors that place limits on it: ignorance and force (or, more positively, knowledge and freedom). We have already dealt fairly extensively with ignorance. We said, for instance, that if someone does not know what sacrilege is—and this ignorance is not the result of negligence—then he cannot commit the crime of sacrilege. Ignorance of circumstances can also limit culpability. Although Oedipus killed his father, Laius, since he did not know who he was ("who" being the relevant circumstance), he did not commit the crime of parricide. But what about force? There is still quite a bit to say about force—or, at least, about what it points to—and about the way in which this factor characterizes the intelligible subject matter that is the basis of morality.

The classic definition of exonerating force, formulated by Aristotle and taken over by Thomas Aquinas, is "that of which the initiative is outside, the person involved (whether active or passive) contributing nothing to it."[5] The usual examples employed in explaining this definition have to do with physical force. A man who is pushed onto the trigger beam of a catapult that fires and kills another man does not commit murder, since the moving force behind the act comes from outside and he contributes nothing to it. But although such examples are the paradigm examples of exonerating force, indicating causes independent of the will of the person in question, the same general factor (being independent of the will) enters into the analysis of human action in another way. When a person performs an action

5. *EN* iii.1.1110a1–3; in Thomas, see *ST* 1-2.6.4–6.

previously and correctly defined as a good action of a certain type, his will is not tied up in that action's being what it is.

I mentioned in chapter 1 that the contours of natural law can be seen not only in man's natural inclinations, such as the inclination to remain in existence or to reproduce, but also in the way he organizes the communities in which he lives. Near the beginning of the present chapter I noted that things subject to natural law, such as societies, are in accordance with it to the extent that they reflect, as best they are able, its intelligibility. The perfect intelligibility of natural law channels and shapes, to the extent possible, the practices of a just society. We might call these practices "fixed paths."

Take, for example, medicine. It is part of man's nature to establish a medical profession. In whatever society one considers, provided it is large enough, certain individuals eventually come to be recognized as doctors. (This does not happen among cows or horses or even bees; we are talking about natural law as it pertains to rational beings: men and women.) These doctors will employ certain standard procedures. If we are to say that these procedures are consistent with natural law, we must assume that the medical profession to which they belong has progressed as far as reasonably possible. That profession's procedures must also be consistent with the nature of medicine itself; in particular, it can contain no procedure that contradicts medicine's fundamental principle of doing no harm to the patient. Given such a well-conducted medical profession, we can speak of procedures that, to the best of medical knowledge, are both in accordance with natural law and are independent of the wills of the doctors who perform them.

Consider, for example, the following standard case in medical ethics. A pregnant woman's uterus is infected with cancer. According to the church's moral teaching (and natural law), provided that it is the only way of preserving the life of the mother, removal of the cancerous uterus (a hysterectomy) is permissible, even though, as the doctor knew beforehand would happen, the baby dies as a result.

Consider another case: a pregnant woman's constitution is such that her life will be threatened if she carries her baby to term; a doctor suggests that the early fetus be dissolved with chemicals. The church has said (of similar procedures) that such a procedure is not in accordance with natural law. What is the difference?

The difference is that hysterectomy is a standard procedure in sound medical practice; dissolving a fetus with chemicals is not. How can we know this? In order to distinguish the two procedures, one begins with what it is to be a medical procedure. The craft of medicine is made up essentially of intentional physical movements—human actions—performed upon patients. A doctor does attend conferences, fill out insurance forms, and give advice, and when he does such things he might be acting as a doctor, but it is physical movements performed upon patients that define the craft of medicine.

As Aristotle explains in his *Physics,* a physical movement always has a physical object: some physical state toward which it proceeds and that contributes to its "species" (or type). A cylinder's rolling down an incline has as its object (even when the rolling is not fully accomplished) the bottom of the incline or "being at the bottom of the incline"; hitting a baseball has as its object the baseball—or, perhaps better, the ball's being within the area defined by the two foul lines in such a way that no opposing player catches it. What gives movements their species is their objects *as* standing at the end of a movement of a certain type: the bottom of the incline considered as the finishing point of a rolling, the baseball as hit by a baseball player wielding a baseball bat. Although a baseball's being hit is more than just a baseball (presupposing, as it does, the whole game of baseball), the hitting of a baseball does not occur without the baseball. Similarly, medical actions in order to be medical actions must (and do) have physical objects. So, the species of a medical procedure is bound up with the patient at which it is directed—or with the particular organ operated upon *as* belonging to the patient. It has to do also with doing good for that object. Medicine is defined by its sound procedures, not by its illicit ones—that is, those that violate the principle, "Do no harm to the patient."

We have now enough theory in place to say why the hysterectomy even of a pregnant uterus can be moral, while dissolving a fetus with chemicals cannot be. The object of a hysterectomy is a woman's uterus: that is what is found at the end of the single physical action called "hysterectomy." That the woman and her uterus are both within the object becomes apparent in attending to the fact that the idea of performing the procedure *just* upon the uterus makes no sense at all. The idea is to get the woman into a healthy state by removing her uterus. These characteristics of the procedure are established well before the arrival of a fetus in the uterus to be operated upon, for "hysterectomy" is defined—has its intelligibility—independently of the presence of that fetus. So, when a doctor performs a hysterectomy even upon a pregnant woman, his object can be the woman (or, perhaps, "the woman brought into a healthy state by the removal of her uterus").

On the other hand, the object of dissolving a fetus with chemicals is a fetus. It is true that that particular physical act has as a further object a healthy woman, but the intellect is not free to look away from the act that has as its object the fetus and to say that this is just an act upon the woman. In other words, the person evaluating such procedures is not free to declare that saving the mother by first killing her fetus does not have two features that need to be taken into account. Unlike a hysterectomy, which is a single unit of intelligibility concluding in a woman's uterus being removed in order to do her good, dissolving a fetus with chemicals is a single unit of intelligibility concluding in an object—a fetus—for which it clearly does no good. Of course, this physical act fits into a larger piece of intelligibility: dissolving the fetus in order to save the mother; but it has an intelligibility (or lack of intelligibility) all its own.

The legitimacy of describing a hysterectomy as a single piece of intelligibility is bound up with its being a genuine medical procedure: a fixed path. Medical manuals, in describing medical operations, describe units of intelligibility; that operation would be included in any complete and genuine medical manual. Someone might object: Why then not just include "fetal dissolution" as a medical procedure? But that would not be possible since, as we have seen, a fundamental principle of medicine is "do no harm to the patient" (that is, to the object of a particular medical procedure). Obviously, such a procedure could be inserted into a medical manual of some sort; but its insertion would be illegitimate if the manual includes—as a fully intelligible medical manual must—the principle, "Do no harm to the patient."

We shall come back to these issues in chapters 4 and 7.

three

MORAL ABSOLUTES, SEXUAL MORALITY, REPRODUCTIVE ETHICS

In this chapter I consider two areas of concern that are related to each other: sexual ethics and reproductive bioethics. The church's teaching in both areas has borne controversy with it. The controversy is unavoidable since, by the grace of God, the church's moral teaching more closely approximates eternal law than can any ethical theory that depends upon human reasoning alone. Given man's fallen state, human reason supported by divine grace cannot help but come up with answers to moral questions different from the answers put forward by human reason left to its own devices, especially where there are personal interests and desires involved. Nor is controversy necessarily a thing to be avoided, for, where there is controversy, obviously there are things that need to be sorted out. The test of a theory is in how well it performs this task.

In the previous chapter we spoke of one way of breaking down a human action into parts: by looking to its object, intention, and at least some of its circumstances. But there are other junctures at which we might break down an action into parts. Consider again the man who steals the golden cup from the temple. That is one action, the full moral character of which is determined by its object (the cup), its intention (whatever that may be), and the circumstance that the cup is found in a temple. But we can also isolate a very basic segment of that action: the *stealing*. Although the idea of stealing presupposes a number of other ideas—such as the idea "property," the idea "of another" (as in "property of another"), and the idea "taking"—as a morally significant act, a stealing is quite simple. It is the taking of that which belongs to another, independently of such added factors as that the cup is found in a temple or, for example, that the act is done to insult a group of people or with hopes of igniting a war. The stealing is that to which these other things are added.

Morally, the distinctive characteristic of the basic segment "stealing" is that it contains in itself a rupture of practical intelligibility—that is, of intelligibility *qua* good thing to do. The positive correlate of taking what is not one's own is taking or having what is one's own. This latter is in itself good and, as such, is completely intelligible. When a man receives a new hammer in the mail and delights simply in having it, it is a pure delight, corresponding to a natural human inclination to have things. This is not to say that there might not be other considerations that make that having bad—the man may be taking possession of the hammer in order to commit a crime or in violation of a vow he has made—but the pure delight in having corresponds to a basic and good natural inclination. Stealing gets what intelligibility it has from "good having" by negating or perverting it: a person takes what is *not* his own. Stealing, in other words, is the dark flip side of good having. It is always wrong, since it is the negation of a basic and simple piece of intelligibility: having what is one's own.

Similarly, telling a lie is the dark flip side of telling the truth. It gets what intelligibility it has from truth telling, but only by going directly against it. As with having what is one's own, telling the truth can involve added factors that make it a bad thing to do—this particular moment may not be the best moment to tell someone that his wife is unfaithful—but truth telling in itself is good. To go against truth is always to do something that attacks intelligibility and is therefore unreasonable. Telling the truth, therefore, is in itself good, but sometimes bad; lying is always bad, no matter what the added factors.

That, then, is what intrinsically bad acts are: the negations—we might also say, "perversions"—of simple segments of intelligibility. As almost everyone knows, the church identifies a number of intrinsically bad acts in the field of sexual ethics: masturbation, for example, the various types of contraception, sodomy, fornication, and adultery. (One must also mention here "conceiving a child *in vitro*" or by means of some other method of artificial fertilization—although this type of act presents special considerations, to be considered below.) Such acts are intrinsically immoral because they go against a basic segment of intelligibility.

What is it that masturbation, contraception, sodomy go against? The conjugal (or marital) act. Since the conjugal act constitutes the core intelligibility of sexuality, any sexual activity that is not sexual activity between a man and his wife is intrinsically wrong. Conjugal intercourse is the norm for all human sexuality—which is to say that it is the only sexual activity that can be moral: any deviation from this norm is a deviation from intelligibility. The most basic segment of intelligibility here is not, therefore, intercourse *per se*—that is, that sexual activity engaged in both by man and certain animals, nor even that engaged in both by spouses and non-spouses, but intercourse between a man and his wife. Morality is about doing that which is reasonable, and marriage is man's way of ordering sexuality (and other activities connected to it) in a reasonable way.

Is it possible to be more specific about the characteristics of the conjugal act, so that we might say in a precise manner what type of acts fall short of it? It is. A useful document for doing this is a decree published in 1977 by the Congregation for the Doctrine of the Faith; its title is simply, "Regarding Impotence That Invalidates Marriage."

The decree is useful, since it represents not just a procedural ruling in canon law, but an authoritative interpretation of natural law. The issue that the decree decided was whether a man who during sexual intercourse can emit seminal fluid, but whose seminal fluid does not contain sperm, can consummate a marriage. In ecclesiastical courts prior to the decree, the practice was to consider such men not capable of consummating marriage. The decree countermanded this practice; in effect, it separated—with respect to the consummation of marriage—the issue of the physical union of the two spouses from the issue of procreation or possible fecundity. What was necessary was not semen capable of bringing about conception, but rather, and merely, ejaculation into the vagina. This entails that sexual intercourse during which the male makes use of a prophylactic (or condom) is intrinsically wrong, since it deliberately prevents the potentially marital act from being a marital act at all: it prevents it, that is, from arriving at its object, which is the seminal fluid deposited in the vagina. Use of a prophylactic is wrong even if it is not for contraceptive purposes, since it prevents a true one-flesh union between the spouses.[1]

There is more to say, of course, about the proper characteristics of the conjugal act. To say, as I have done, that the issue of the physical union of the two spouses is separate from the issue of procreation

---

1. The decree does not say explicitly that intercourse with a condom impedes performance of the conjugal act; but if the church were ever to say (what I do not believe it ever will say) that intercourse using a condom can be a conjugal act, it would be rendering the decree null, since the latter would never have been issued had this been an ethical possibility. The decree was issued as a consequence of programs of forced vasectomy instituted during the early twentieth century by various European governments. Men so dealt with could still emit in the sexual act an ejaculate, although the fluid contained no sperm and so was incapable of bringing about conception. The whole controversy was over the *character* of "semination within the vagina" [*seminatio intra vaginam*]. It was presupposed that semination was required; the question was just whether semination required the presence of sperm. It would be illicit to argue that semination could be "within" the vagina, even if the man wears a condom during the sexual act, for, if *that* counted as semination within the vagina, the issue of the presence of sperm would never have been posed.

is not to say that openness to procreation is not also an essential characteristic of true conjugal intercourse. The document most useful for establishing this latter point is Paul VI's 1968 encyclical letter *Humanae vitae,* where we are taught that "the first principles of the human Christian doctrine of marriage" exclude as immoral "any action that—when marital intercourse is either foreseen, engaged in, or proceeding toward its natural consequences—intends, either as an end to be obtained or as a course of action to be pursued, that procreation be impeded" [§14]. *Humanae vitae* speaks throughout (as in this quotation) not about sexuality itself, but about marriage; but this is entirely appropriate since, as we have seen, the conjugal act is the standard for all sexual activity.

The essential characteristics of the conjugal act are given succinct formulation in the church's Code of Canon Law—in particular, in section 1 of canon 1061—where we are told that a marriage has been consummated "if the spouses have performed between themselves in a human fashion a conjugal act that is suitable in itself for the procreation of offspring, to which marriage is ordered by its nature and by which the spouses become one flesh." Despite a certain verbal resemblance to a remark in Vatican II's *Gaudium et spes* [§49] about love "expressed in a manner which is truly human" and that speaks also about "mutual self-giving by which spouses enrich each other with a joyful and a ready will," the phrase "in a human fashion" in canon 1061, §1 does not refer to acts as characterized in this manner, but simply to acts as characterized as "human" in the philosophical sense of performed knowingly and without coercion. If an act of sexual intercourse between two spouses is not an expression of joy and *ready* will, it may very well be the result of sinful action, but it can nonetheless be an act of conjugal intercourse.

The clause about the conjugal act's being "suitable in itself for the procreation of offspring" does not mean that, for instance, a sterile couple cannot consummate marriage, but rather that even they, in order to do so, must perform an act of the *type* that would lead to procreation if they were not sterile. This would certainly exclude the possibility of consummating marriage by means of unnatural intercourse (such as anal intercourse) or by means of intercourse during which a prophylactic is used. Neither of these would constitute the spouses' becoming "one flesh." Whether the use of oral contraceptives (which do not interfere with the conjugal act itself) impedes the consummation of marriage is an issue that remains disputed by moral theologians and canon lawyers. My own opinion is that it does not, since the act of intercourse, which receives its species (its "what it is") from its object (seminal fluid deposited in the vagina), is, in orally contracepted intercourse, brought to completion. This is not to say, however, that oral contraception is moral; on the contrary, it is immoral, because it goes against an essential property of the marital act: openness to procreation.

As I have already suggested, some of the consequences of this teaching—not to mention the teaching itself—are controversial; not, however, in the sense that they are doubtful, but in the sense that they are not readily accepted in a culture ideologically committed to resisting any limitations on sexual activity. One such consequence is that the use of prophylactics in order to prevent the spread of diseases such as HIV and AIDS is excluded—although on varying grounds, depending on the situation. If the question is whether two male homosexuals ought to use a prophylactic during sexual relations, the answer is that they ought not to be engaging in homosexual acts in the first place: if they did what was moral, there would be no reason to use prophylactics. The men ought not to be engaging in homosexual acts, since such acts are (obviously) not conjugal acts.

But—and here we get even more controversial—prophylactics ought not to be employed, even when the intercourse contemplated is between spouses. There are various reasons for insisting on this. One would be the known ineffectiveness of prophylactics in preventing the transmission of diseases such as HIV and AIDS. By this I do not mean that they are *totally* ineffective: prophylactics do certainly reduce the rate of transmission of such diseases, but they are not 100-percent effective. For a man with HIV or AIDS to have intercourse with his wife knowing that there is (say) one chance in a hundred that the prophylactic he uses will not be effective is to play Russian roulette—but with his *wife*'s head at the other end of the gun, not his own. It is impossible to see such an act as an act of love; it is an act, rather, of gross selfishness.

But let us suppose that science or technology could develop a prophylactic that was 100-percent effective. Even still, the use of this prophylactic would be immoral, since it would stand in the way of the one-flesh union of man and wife. The intercourse engaged in would not be conjugal intercourse. Since any sexual activity that deviates from conjugal intercourse is immoral, the use of prophylactics in this (admittedly) hypothetical situation would be immoral.

Above (in chapter 2) I mentioned that a lie is always immoral, since it is the perversion of a basic unit of intelligibility—in this case, truth telling. The case of the married couple with AIDS can be likened to the much-discussed case of the person faced with Nazis at the door who ask whether there are Jews within. Both are, in the technical sense, "hard cases": cases that help us to evaluate theories. Following especially St. Augustine, the church has always insisted that lying is prohibited, even in such circumstances (although it is permissible to *mislead* the Nazis). Similarly, the church does not permit the use of condoms even for married couples with AIDS, since one-flesh union is necessary in order for there to be a moral sexual act. Both these cases apply pressure at what appear to be weak points in a larger theory. But actually, the points at which the pressure is applied are as strong as theoretical points can get, since they refer to that which is utterly simple and compact. The basic segments of intelligibility referred to in either case are clearly good things: truth telling and natural intercourse between spouses in which they truly become one flesh. The deviations from these acts have the significance they have only because they are associated with the acts—*as* deviations.

To conclude this chapter, I would like consider some issues in reproductive bioethics. Doing so in the present context, besides providing some insight into the issues themselves, will allow us to see the interconnected character of the principles of natural law ethics—which are, of course, also the principles of the church's ethical teaching. But, before getting into the substance of these bioethical issues, we shall have need of a couple of preliminary points.

In the early 1960s, even before the publication of *Humanae vitae,* there was a good deal of discussion among Catholic scholars regarding the morality of contraception. Some, of course, would eventually maintain that the use of contraception was not intrinsically immoral; but even among the teachings' defenders, there was dissatisfaction with some of the philosophical arguments used to defend it. One such argument was that contraception was immoral because it prevented a natural function from achieving its natural end. Certain scholars rejected this reasoning, arguing that it proved too much: it would make immoral the use of earplugs, for instance, since they impede ears from hearing things, which is their natural end. So, an alternative explanation was formulated, according to which contraception is immoral because it attacks the basic good of human life. Obviously, contraception does not attack human life in the way that abortion does; it does, however, attack potential human life and that (according to this account) is enough to make the act immoral.

The problem is that, traditionally, contraception has always been considered a sin against the sixth commandment ("Thou shalt not commit adultery"), and this other approach makes it not a sexual sin, but a sin against the fifth commandment, "Thou shalt not kill." In presenting contraception as a deviation from the conjugal act, *Humanae vitae* in effect takes the traditional approach. So does more recent church teaching. In the *Catechism of the Catholic Church* contraception is treated in the section devoted to the sixth commandment; and in *Evangelium vitae,* John Paul II writes as follows:

Certainly, from the moral point of view contraception and abortion are specifically different evils: the former contradicts the full truth of the sexual act as the proper expression of conjugal love, while the latter destroys the life of a human being; the former is opposed to the virtue of chastity in marriage, the latter is opposed to the virtue of justice and directly violates the divine commandment "You shall not kill" [§13].

It would seem, therefore, that the immorality of contraception is better understood as a deviation from the norm for sexual behavior, the conjugal act. This understanding is more in accord with church teaching and, like the "contraception is anti-life" argument, does not entail absurdities such as the immorality of ear plugs, since wearing earplugs has nothing intrinsically to do with the conjugal act. The conjugal act is not unrelated to human life issues, since that act must be the type of act suitable for the procreation of offspring; but, within the conjugal act, this aspect is bound together with the unitive aspect, whereby man and wife achieve one-flesh unity in the way specified by their Creator.

This approach has the advantage that it also provides a way of explaining the church's teaching on artificial fertilization, such as "*in vitro* fertilization" or any other method of conceiving babies independently of the conjugal act. People—even good Catholics—very reasonably ask, if human life is a good thing, why *not* bring it about that there is more of it? Why *not* bring it about that this couple, who otherwise cannot conceive, might have and raise their own child? If one does not assume that the conjugal act, which both unites the spouses and is open to procreation, serves as the norm also here, such arguments are very persuasive. But if one does assume that the conjugal act is determinative here, such arguments lose much of their persuasive force.

The Congregation for the Doctrine of the Faith's *Donum vitae* says that contraception is wrong because it "deprives the conjugal act of its openness to procreation and in this way brings about a voluntary dissociation of the ends of marriage" (that is, procreation and one-flesh unity of the spouses). It then says that artificial fertilization "in seeking a procreation which is not the fruit of a specific act of conjugal union, objectively effects an analogous separation between the goods and the meanings of marriage" [§4(a)]. The church points, therefore, to a very important parallel: contraception cuts procreation away from sexual intercourse, artificial fertilization cuts sexual intercourse away from procreation. The same central normative act that serves to establish the intrinsic immorality of nonconjugal sexual activity serves also to establish the intrinsic immorality of artificial fertilization—which might similarly be called nonconjugal and be repudiated as such.

This link between the conjugal act and the bioethics of procreation gives us some insight into an issue that some claim is left unresolved in *Donum vitae* and in the subsequent related document, *Dignitas personae*. *Donum vitae* quotes a definition by Pope Pius XII of the conjugal act:

> In its natural structure, the conjugal act is a personal action, a simultaneous and immediate cooperation on the part of the husband and wife, which by the very nature of the agents and the proper nature of the act is the expression of the mutual gift that, according to the words of Scripture, brings about union "in one flesh."[2]

Donum vitae associates this definition with another remark, also by Pius XII, but in another document, to the effect that morality "does not necessarily proscribe the use of artificial means intended solely either to facilitate the natural act or to enable the natural act performed in a normal manner to attain its end."[3] (The term "facilitate" used here must be understood as meaning that a particular act is enabled to do its job in such a way that some other act does not

2. This is from an address in 1949 to the Italian Union of Catholic Midwives [AAS 43 (1951): 850]; it is quoted in *Donum vitae* at II.B.6 [AAS 80 (1988): 95].

3. "Address to the Fourth International Congress of Catholic Doctors," September 29, 1949 [AAS 41 (1949): 560]; quoted in *Donum vitae* at II.B.6 [AAS 80 (1988): 95].

substitute for it.) On this doctrinal basis, *Donum vitae* concludes: "If the technical means facilitates the conjugal act or helps it to reach its natural objectives, it can be morally acceptable. If, on the other hand, the procedure were to replace the conjugal act, it would be morally illicit."

This remark has been interpreted as leaving the door open for procedures such as GIFT (Gamete Intra-Fallopian Transfer). In this procedure the sperm and eggs of a man and a woman having difficulty conceiving are washed and then placed via a catheter directly into the woman's fallopian tubes; fertilization occurs inside the woman's body. If such a procedure is to be considered even *possibly* licit, the sperm must be obtained through the use of a perforated condom (which allows for one-flesh unity), and the sperm and eggs must be those of a married couple (the couple undergoing the whole procedure). Some scholars argue that such a procedure is licit, since it is adopted simply in order to facilitate the conjugal act or to allow "the natural act performed in a normal manner to attain its end."

But it seems to me that such a procedure does (in the word of *Donum vitae*) "replace" the conjugal act and is therefore immoral. As a human action, the conjugal act receives its species from its object: the deposit of sperm in the vagina. Like all such physical acts, its end point is quite precisely identifiable: once the sperm is deposited, the conjugal act is finished. Some scholars resist this conclusion, since they fear that it is to understand the conjugal act in a "physicalist" way; but we have already seen (in chapter 2) that such fears are groundless.

Let me use some rather bizarre examples that will (I hope) bring the pertinent issues into relief. Imagine a wind machine blowing beach balls toward a target. If there were some man nudging the balls past obstacles so that they could continue toward the target, the action causing the balls to get to the target would be that of the machine; the helper's action would be a facilitation of the machine's action. What counts here is that the impetus from the machine is what gets the balls to the target. If the machine were too weak to get the balls to the target and the man were to kick them to the target, he would become the cause of their getting there.

The example of the machine and the beach balls does not in fact correspond to what occurs in the conjugal act. Sperm are not like beach balls, because the impetus getting them to their target does not come from the male partner in the conjugal act. His part in the act gets things going, of course, but the sperm have their own movements about which the male knows nothing and that he cannot affect. (Aristotle, by the way, got this wrong: he thought that insemination was a matter of the male's original impetus continuing until the embryo began moving on its own.) It is more like a man's releasing a bunch of small animals (dogs, let's say) in the direction of a target. Suppose that the dogs get trapped in some way, a keeper frees them from the traps, gives them a meal, and then leads them to a place before the target. The act of the keeper does help along the general project of the person originally releasing the dogs, but it is not a facilitating of that act of releasing the dogs. It is the keeper who now releases the dogs toward the target. This is a new releasing; the original releasing is over and done with.

GIFT can be compared to this latter case. The keeper is doing what the other man hoped to accomplish, but what the keeper is doing is a distinct act. Similarly, the conjugal act involves sending out sperm, which then do what they do by nature (swim). What the technicians are doing is helping the sperm to swim to the target; they are not facilitating the conjugal act, which isn't tied in any essential way to the action of sperm.

The only type of facilitating of the conjugal act that seems to me to be possible under *Donum vitae* would be either procedures that occur well before the conjugal act in order to make sure that fecundation is not impeded or operations that have certainly never been done and probably never will be done. If, for instance, there were a flap of tissue in between the place where the semen is first placed in the woman and the location of the ova, and this tissue were to come down occasionally and block the way, it would be legitimate to go in there and, at the appropriate time, lift the flap up so that the sperm could get by. If this was done *within* the woman's body itself (the compounded "if" clauses make the prospect more and more unlikely), it seems to me that it could be considered a facilitation of the conjugal act. But a procedure such as GIFT replaces the conjugal act and is, therefore, morally illicit.

four

THE ETHICS OF KILLING

The ethics of killing is more complicated than sexual ethics. As we saw in the previous chapter, all of sexual ethics (and also the ethics of artificial fertilization) depends upon a single positive act—the conjugal act—considered normative, so that determining whether a relevant act is moral is simply a matter of looking to see whether it is a deviation from the conjugal act. Determining whether an act of killing is moral is not so easy. According to church teaching, murder is always immoral, while killing in war is usually moral; killing in personal self-defense is usually moral, but probably not for the same reasons as killing in war; and capital punishment is usually immoral.

The reason for this complexity is that the ethics of killing lacks a single positive act functioning as the norm. This changes the way this sector of ethics works logically. If there were such a normative act, it would be the "act" of living; but, strictly speaking, we cannot even refer to this as an act (that is, a human act), since in itself it does not involve the intention to *do* anything.

The governing factor in the ethics of killing is not a single normative act, but rather a sort of default principle—"Avoid taking life"—whose scope is specified by other considerations. How do we recognize a legitimate specification of this scope? We must look to what human reason, working not independently of divine aid, recognizes as reasonable. It is reasonable and good to avoid taking human life, but it is unreasonable, for instance, to be a total pacifist, since that would entail neglecting duties toward family, friends, and society. The specification of the default principle "avoid taking life"—the establishment of rules for the legitimate use of lethal force, for instance—has been the concern of legislators and jurists from time immemorial. This work has involved and continues to involve formulating laws and, given changed circumstances and increased knowledge, testing them for consistency and justice. To the extent that human law attains these latter qualities, it reflects the perfect consistency and justice of natural law and eternal law (see chapter 1).

But, if it is true that there is no single human act to serve as the focal point for the ethics of killing, there is a convenient central text: Thomas Aquinas's *Summa theologiae* 2-2.64.7. It is a rare treatment of killing, whether by the magisterium or by Catholic scholars, that does not make reference to this article. The body of the article, which I have divided into two sections, the second much shorter than the first, runs as follows:[1]

> Nothing hinders one act from having two effects, only one of which is intended, while the other is beside the intention. Now moral acts take their species according to what is intended, and not according to what is beside the intention, since this is accidental, as explained above.[2] Accordingly, the act of self-defense may have two effects: one is the saving of one's life, the other is the slaying of the aggressor. Therefore this act, since one's intention is to save one's own life, is not unlawful, seeing that it is natural to everything to keep itself in being, as far as possible. And yet, though proceeding from a good inten-

1. The modern translation of the *Summa theologiae* comes from *Thomas Aquinas, Summa Theologica,* translated by the Fathers of the English Dominican Province (London: Burns, Oates and Washbourne, 1920); see the appendix, "Bibliographical Matters."
2. Thomas is apparently referring to *ST* 2-2.59.2; 2-2.43.3; and 1-2.72.1; see also (later) *ST* 2-2.69.4.

tion, an act may be rendered unlawful if it is out of proportion to the end. Wherefore if a man, in self-defense, uses more than necessary violence, it will be unlawful: whereas if he repel force with moderation his defense will be lawful, because, according to the jurists, "it is lawful to repel force by force, provided one does not exceed the limits of a blameless defense." Nor is it necessary for salvation that a man omit the act of moderate self-defense in order to avoid killing the other man, since one is bound to take more care of one's own life than of another's.

But as it is unlawful to take a man's life, except for the public authority acting for the common good, as stated above,[3] it is not lawful for a man to intend killing a man in self-defense, except for such as have public authority, who while intending to kill a man in self-defense, refer this to the public good, as in the case of a soldier fighting against the foe, and in the minister of the judge struggling with robbers, although even these sin if they be moved by private animosity.

Aquinas is saying here, first of all, that it is sometimes licit to perform an act of personal self-defense. An act can have two effects, only one of which is intended, as when a private citizen defends himself from an attacker, intending only to save his own life, accepting the death of his assailant as a side effect. The "moral species" of any act ("what it is" morally that the person is doing) comes from what the act primarily tends toward (in this case, saving one's own life), not that which is "beside the intention" (the death of the attacker). An act of killing in self-defense simply so described is licit, since "it is natural to everything to keep itself in being, as far as possible."

Sometimes, however, an act belonging to this general category is illicit because the instrument the agent employs is disproportionate to the purpose of protecting his own life. A man knows that he can deter an aggressor by using a less powerful weapon, but chooses a more powerful one. Aquinas does not say whether such an act remains an act of self-defense, or whether it becomes an act of another

3. Thomas is apparently referring to ST 2-2.64.3.

type: simple murder. He says only that "though proceeding *from* a good intention, an act may be *rendered* unlawful, if it be out of proportion to the end." But we can provide an interpretation of Thomas's remarks that is consistent with his more general principles. It could be that, having decided to defend himself, the man deliberately chooses a weapon that is clearly lethal, although there was a less—but sufficiently—powerful weapon available. In this case, his action would no longer be self-defense, but murder. Or it could be that neither weapon is clearly lethal, although one is more likely to kill—and the man chooses this weapon heedless of whether the attacker lives or dies. In this latter case, the act remains an act of self-defense: self-defense "rendered immoral," however, by the man's heedless choice of means. Human law supports this general approach, for (as Thomas notes) it says that "it is lawful to repel force by force, *provided* one does not exceed the limits of a blameless defense."[4]

So far, then, we have three cases: (1) licit self-defense (in which the proportionate means could be a lethal weapon, if that is all that is available); (2) self-defense that turns into murder (because the agent chooses clearly lethal means when less powerful but proportionate means are available); and (3) illicit self-defense (in which the agent could have chosen proportionate and nonlethal means, but is heedless). In all three cases, the choosing of the weapon is a human act. There is no suggestion in what Aquinas says that the choice and use of the means are not intentional, even though the *death* of the assailant may be "beside the intention," so that the act falls under the species "self-defense."

Having discussed in the longer first part of *ST* 2-2.64.7, at least primarily, acts in which the death of the assailant is beside the intention, in the second section Aquinas turns explicitly to acts in which the killing is not beside the intention (once again: the intention *as*

---

4. Aquinas is quoting the *Decretals* of Pope Gregory IX. He appears also to be invoking divine law in this regard, for he adds that it is not "necessary for salvation" to omit such an act of self-defense.

determining the species of the act). A man who is deputed by public authority to kill for the sake of the common good, provided that he is not moved by private animosity, kills licitly. Aquinas gives an example of a soldier who, in defending himself, kills a foe. He contrasts such a man with a private individual who intends to kill. He has in mind a man who performs an act similar to that of a soldier, but without the public authority. He acts immorally.

That is the basic argument of *ST* 2-2.64.7. There are a number of things about the article well worth attending to. First, according to Aquinas, killing a human being is not an intrinsically immoral act, as is, for instance, lying. Although murder is intrinsically immoral, killing a man is sometimes a reasonable thing to do. Second, Aquinas's immediate grounds for saying what he says in the article are not the distinction between intending and not intending; his immediate grounds are, rather, legal. He cites positive human law a number of times, although he also acknowledges that the relevant positive human laws are consistent with natural law. Third, one notices that the scope of Aquinas's concern in *ST* 2-2.64.7 is quite limited. In the first section of the article, he speaks primarily of defense of oneself, saying nothing, for instance, about a private citizen who might need to defend his wife or children. In the second section, about publicly sanctioned killing, Aquinas speaks of a soldier or other civil officer who is, again, defending *himself.*

Points one and two are connected with what we said above about the particular logic of the ethics of killing. Killing a person not being an intrinsically immoral act is a consequence of there being no single normative case against which all acts in this sector of ethics are to be measured. There is a general presumption in natural law that preserving life is to be preferred, but there are types of killing that are reasonable and just. How do we know which types these are? Although Aquinas had in his workshop the concepts of intention, object, species, and so on, his first instinct in assessing the morality of killing was not to invoke them, but to reach for his law books. Not that the

ethics of killing depends solely on human law, either: such a methodology would finish in relativism. Aquinas rather follows Aristotle's
methodology of examining first the most reputable ethical opinions
available (especially the opinions that respectable legislators put into
laws) and then subjecting them to critical analysis to see whether
they are self-consistent and sound—in short, to see whether they can
be consonant with natural and (ultimately) eternal law. Such critical
analyses have also been performed by legislators or scholars before
Aquinas, who have had in their workshop many of the same tools as
he; in *ST* 2-2.64.7, Aquinas does not hesitate to avail himself of their
analyses and results.

Point three, having to do with *ST* 2-2.64.7's being limited to self-
defense, indicates that a more complete ethics of killing, such as we
are presenting here, will involve extrapolating from what Aquinas
says in order to determine the morality of types of acts not considered there. For instance, although *ST* 2-2.64.7 is primarily about a
man's defending himself, it is reasonable to extend what is said there
to his killing in defense of someone in his care, such as a wife or
children. The idea that self-defense can be legitimate inasmuch as it
derives its species only from what is intended—that is, saving life—
remains valid. If a man knows, for instance, that his neighbor has
killed his daughter and so, taking the law into his own hands, enters
his house and beats him up or even kills him, his act is not one of
self-defense, because its intention is not to protect an attacked life,
but to do harm or to kill. But a man might licitly harm or kill the
neighbor as the latter attacks his daughter, provided there is no other
way of preserving her life or bodily integrity.

Aquinas's remarks about proportionate and disproportionate
means must be extrapolated similarly. The moral considerations are
the same if an agent is, for instance, protecting his family from an in-
truder. If a man chooses a weapon that is clearly lethal when another
less—but sufficiently—powerful weapon is available, he has moved
into a different moral zone: not defense of his family, but murder in

some degree. As before, if the available weapons are not clearly lethal but he is heedless of the possibility of taking another's life and
chooses the more powerful when a less powerful weapon would have
sufficed, his act remains one of defending his family, but has been
rendered immoral by his heedlessness.

Let us consider now killing performed by a soldier, as an example
of a public official. Here too a bit of extrapolation—or perhaps better explanation—is required. As mentioned, Aquinas speaks in *ST*
2-2.64.7 of the soldier who kills a foe while defending himself. But
here the self-defense aspect is not essential for the analysis of what a
soldier does. A soldier behind battlements operating a catapult does
not fear for his life and yet, in operating the catapult, which is a lethal
instrument, he acts as a soldier. Unlike the private self-defender, a
soldier's act does receive its species—what it is—from an intention
to kill, or at least possibly to kill, plus the further intention, to which
all soldiers' acts are necessarily linked as long as they remain soldiers' acts, of protecting the common good. Why then in *ST* 2-2.64.7
does Aquinas speak of the soldier or other public official as defending himself?—simply because that article is about self-defense. In the
present context, however, in which we are considering the ethics of
killing more generally, such limits are not appropriate. We can ex-
trapolate and apply what Aquinas says in *ST* 2-2.64.7 to any soldiers
acting as soldiers. A soldier acting as a soldier and killing a person
intentionally behaves morally as long as he is not "moved by private
animosity," private animosity not being part of the intelligibility of his
acting as soldier.

Let us now move even further away from *ST* 2-2.64.7 (without,
however, cutting loose from it entirely) and consider soldiers operating as part of an army—for the issues here are obviously also part
of the ethics of killing. Although the analysis of a soldier acting as a
soldier does not involve essentially the idea of self-defense, the analysis of an army does: indeed, the applicable (or extrapolatable) ideas
are basically those of the first section of *ST* 2-2.64.7. The actions of

armies are moral only if they do not involve disproportionate means. If a battle might be won by frightening the enemy out of their wits so that they lay down their arms or run away, that outcome should be preferred to killing them (or killing them all). And, if an enemy soldier lays down his arms, clearly indicating that he wants to surrender, an army cannot order one of its soldiers to kill him, since, at that point, this other person is no longer hostile and, strictly speaking, therefore no longer an enemy soldier. But a general of an army at war need not say to his soldiers, "Kill as few of the enemy as possible; merely wound them, if you can." His soldiers legitimately set out to kill enemy soldiers and not just to stop them. As we have seen, in soldiering, unlike personal self-defense, no moral stigma attaches to intending to kill.

Let us continue to apply the principles set out in *ST* 2-2.64.7 to cases that are farther afield and yet similar in relevant respects. In warlike situations, then, what precisely are an army's—or a country's—responsibilities with respect to noncombatants? This is an especially important question in modern wars and smaller conflicts in which weapons of mass destruction are at the disposal of most combatants. For an action to be a genuine military action, its object must be an enemy combatant or combatants and not civilians or civilian populations. And so an action that targets civilians does not fall into the class of actions—licit and intended killings—treated in the second section of *ST* 2-2.64.7. Nor, it goes without saying, does it fall into the class of actions treated in the first section.

Such immoral actions would include detonating car bombs in civilian environs and bombing civilian populations in order to terrorize or dispirit them. The use, therefore, of most nuclear weapons is immoral—although the so-called "neutron bomb," whose target area is quite narrow, could conceivably be used morally, provided it is used against a military target: soldiers, for instance, or munitions factories. In the latter case (i.e., the bombing of munitions factories), Catholic moral theology has generally allowed that this can be moral, even if it is known that there are civilians in or near the factories. In such cases it is clear that the object is military; the civilian deaths are "beside the intention" of the military personnel carrying out the strike and of their superiors. The expression "collateral damage"—literally "with, but to the side"—means just that. One sees here the influence of *ST* 2-2.64.7: both of the second section, about the legitimate intentional killing by (for instance) soldiers, and of the first section, about certain effects of actions being "beside the intention."

All this talk of war raises the issue of just and unjust wars. At least since the time of Augustine of Hippo, Christians have taught, with varying degrees of authority, that a war can be just if it satisfies certain criteria; similar criteria are found also in Cicero. The *Catechism of the Catholic Church* [§2309] sets out the following criteria:

- the damage inflicted by the aggressor on the nation or community of nations must be lasting, grave, and certain;
- all other means of putting an end to it must have been shown to be impractical or ineffective;
- there must be the serious prospect of a favorable outcome;
- the use of arms must not entail evils and disorders graver than the evil to be eliminated.[5]

The *Catechism* also adds that "the evaluation of these conditions for moral legitimacy belongs to the prudential judgment of those who have responsibility for the common good."

There are issues left unaddressed in the *Catechism*'s brief list, such as whether preemptive war is necessarily immoral and who can wage a just war (whether, for instance, it might be a group of revolutionaries); but what it says is enough to establish a connection with the general principles put forward in *ST* 2-2.64.7—and that can be at least as useful as a longer list of applications. It is notable that, although the *Catechism*'s treatment of just war is about military measures, the

---

5. My translation is slightly different from the official translation.

principles implicit in it are closer to those of the first section of *ST* 2-2.64.7 than to those of the second. The reason for this is that, in the ethics of killing, whose default principle is "avoid taking life," the presumption is always against war. Before war can be legitimate, the opponent must be truly an aggressor; otherwise, as when a person attacks another who is no real threat, the intention in going to war becomes not defense of the nation, but conquest or simply death to the enemy. Also, the means brought to a just war must be proportionate (as in the first section of *ST* 2-2.64.7)—otherwise, says the *Catechism*, they may bring about "evils and disorders graver than the evil to be eliminated." We might add that the use of disproportionate means would go against the default principle "avoid taking life," which clicks in as destructive means become unnecessary for the task at hand.

The criteria found in the *Catechism*'s list are part of the so-called *ius ad bellum:* international law concerning going to war. There is also a sector of international law called the *ius in bello,* law applying to combatants while fighting. This includes rules we have already seen, such as that genuinely surrendering soldiers ought not to be killed and that noncombatants ought not to be targeted. These latter rules are closely related to the principles of the second section of *ST* 2-2.64.7, for they presume that combatants legitimately intend to kill, that being their justly assigned task. But to whom do these rules apply? Only to those soldiers whose nation wages war justly? When a soldier in an army of an unjust aggressor nation kills his enemy, is that necessarily an immoral act? This need not be so. His act is a military act, and military acts in themselves are in accordance with natural law.

The two areas of international law, *ius ad bellum* and *ius in bello,* are not without a connection between them. The *Catechism* says that the task of declaring war belongs to "those who have responsibility for the common good" and that these authorities "have the right and duty to impose on citizens the obligations necessary for national defense" [§§2309–10]. If a soldier is certain that the authorities had no right or duty to declare a war because it was *not* necessary for the national defense, he would be within his own rights in refusing to serve. The *Catechism* also says that "public authorities should make equitable provision for those who for reasons of conscience refuse to bear arms" [§2311]. A soldier might not be able to say with certainty whether the war in which he fights is a just war. In this case the acts he performs as a soldier are moral, since the task of—and responsibility for—declaring war is assigned specifically to "those who have responsibility for the common good."

A final, related type of killing is capital punishment. Here we have a small problem in the way in which the church has expressed itself in recent years. In the past Catholic theology always acknowledged that capital punishment is in some cases justified. In recent years, concrete societal conditions and attitudes toward capital punishment have altered much, as has church teaching in this regard. The church still teaches that capital punishment is sometimes licit [*Catechism* §2267], although, as part of its general pro-life stance, it discourages recourse to capital punishment much more than it did previously. This is not unreasonable, given the particular logic of the ethics of killing. The scope of the default principle ("avoid taking life") depends upon the concrete political situation in which it has a bearing and upon man's best efforts to organize his society in a way that is consonant with natural and eternal law.

The problem has nothing to do with this development of church teaching. It has to do rather with the fact that, in accounting for the truth of natural law that capital punishment is sometimes licit, the *Catechism* refers not to the second section of *ST* 2-2.64.7 but to the first— that is, to the section about *personal* self-defense. Capital punishment is included under the general rubric "legitimate defense," which latter concept is expounded in terms taken directly from the first section of *ST* 2-2.64.7: "the act of self-defense may have two effects, one is the saving of one's life, the other is the slaying of the aggressor" [*Catechism* §2263].

My point is not that this is an erroneous teaching: in the present chapter, I too have argued that the principles governing the protection of societies need to be extrapolated from that first section of *ST* 2-2.64.7. But the *Catechism* gives the impression that acts of killing by the state can only be understood as legitimate to the extent that they are acts of self-defense, so that the death that results is "beside the intention." But this is not the position of Aquinas, cited three times in this part of the *Catechism* (§§2263–67). As we have seen, in the second section of *ST* 2-2.64.7, he allows that an official of the state can intend to kill. The representation of Aquinas's ideas by the *Catechism* gives the false impression that in the analysis of human action natural law looks only to the intention that a particular agent has in performing an action and not also to the type of action he performs—and to the way it fits into the natural structures of human society: medicine, soldiering, and so forth.

The problem here is simply one of exposition: not the sort of thing that falls under the church's infallibility. The church will continue to teach that capital punishment ought to be used by states only as a last resort. There is no reason it cannot also continue to say that the grounds for (only very rarely) allowing capital punishment is the defense of society. But it would be good if it also represented the fuller doctrine of Aquinas, which allows us to make sense also of other sectors of the natural law.

five

〜

COOPERATION IN EVIL

The badness of the bad acts we have considered thus far has been attributable in a fairly straightforward manner to the agents performing the acts in question. The badness of a man's act of murder, for instance, comes from what *he* has done. But there are many cases in which the badness of one's action comes ultimately from the action of another, the badness of one's own act consisting in one's cooperating with that other bad act. Of course, strictly speaking, moral badness is always the badness of the person who brings it about, but often what is bad about what a person does is that he cooperates in the bad action of another. Understanding such cooperation is essential for dealing with a number of difficult issues of pressing interest to the contemporary church, such as abortion, euthanasia, "homosexual marriage," and stem cell research; so it will be good to say something here about what is traditionally called "cooperation in evil."[1]

A good understanding of cooperation is essential for understand-

---

1. I place the expression "homosexual marriage" here in scare quotes, since no homosexual union can properly be called a marriage. In what follows, however, I drop the scare quotes. Making the point once is sufficient.

ing the responsibilities of legislators, who influence most directly the way societies deal with the issues just mentioned, since the laws they pass—for better or worse—immediately become constitutive parts of the moral world of the people for whom they legislate. To vote for a piece of legislation is not to do the things the legislation permits or even enjoins, but it is often to cooperate in them. If one does not understand this, it becomes quite impossible to make sense of some key ideas in church teaching. In the encyclical letter *Evangelium vitae,* John Paul II says regarding abortion legislation that, "where a legislative vote would be decisive for the passage of a more restrictive law, aimed at limiting the number of authorized abortions, in place of a more permissive law already passed or ready to be voted on," such a vote is permissible, provided the legislator's "absolute personal opposition to procured abortion was well known" [§73]. Now, if voting for a law that permits abortion however restrictively was tantamount morally to procuring an abortion, no legislator could ever vote for such a law; so, the act of voting must be distinct analytically and morally from the acts it would bring about.

An act of voting for a law about abortion has as its object not a fetus in the womb, but rather words to be promulgated as law—and, as we have seen in chapter 2, an act receives its species (its "what it is") from its object. This is not to say, however, that a legislator who, for instance, introduces a law that allows more abortions than previously is not morally culpable for bringing about the deaths of those fetuses: he is. But he does this by means of a vote in favor of (and possibly also by campaigning for) a law—not by dismembering a fetus's skull with a scalpel. Human actions are movements, and obviously the movement of bringing a law into effect is different from the movement effecting an abortion.

A vote in itself is a part of a legislator's job; in itself, therefore, it is a good thing. As we saw in chapter 2, however, an action can be in itself perfectly moral (i.e., as understood in relation to its proper object) and yet be immoral due to circumstances, which include the

reason the act is performed.[2] In the case of the morally upright legislator who votes for a more restrictive abortion law, the reason he
votes for that law is obviously different from that of a legislator who
votes for a less restrictive law. *Qua* acts of voting, therefore, the two
legislators' acts are of the same type; but morally they are quite distinct due to the circumstance that the one is performed with the hope
that abortions will be fewer, the other with the not-displeased expec-
tation that they will be more numerous.[3]

Whether an act of voting is moral or not depends on the type of
cooperation in evil involved, if any. There are two main types: formal
and material.[4] In order for there to be any type, there must be at least
two persons: one person who performs the evil ultimately at issue,
another who cooperates. Of course, there can be more than one primary agent and more than one cooperator, but there must be at least
one of each. A person cooperates formally if (as is sometimes said)
his intention is "mixed up with" the intention of the primary agent
of the evil act; he cooperates only materially if the nature of his act
remains distinct from the intention of the primary agent.

2. In Aristotle, see *EN* iii.1.1111a5; see also Thomas's *ST* 1-2.7.3 ad 3 and *ST* 1-2.18.6 and 9.

3. Elizabeth Anscombe's daughter, Mary Geach, writes in her preface to the Italian translation of *Intention*, G. E. M. Anscombe, *Intenzione* (Rome: Università della Santa Croce, 2004) that what prompted her mother to write the book were "the things which people said in defense of Truman's action in authorizing the bombing of Hiroshima and Nagasaki.... The thing she quoted to me was: 'He only wrote his name on a piece of paper.'" In a note appended to the word "wrote," Geach writes: "Or perhaps she said 'signed.'" My own approach would be closer to Anscombe's than to that of the friends of Truman. Still, my point is not that the legislator who votes in favor of less restrictive abortion legislation is responsible for the actions allowed by the legislation in quite the same way that Truman was responsible for dropping bombs on Hiroshima or Na-gasaki; nor that he is free from moral responsibility for the deaths that result, but that he has not performed any abortions. Nor did Truman drop bombs on Hiroshima or Nagasaki—although he did directly order that those actions be performed.

4. Material cooperation is usually further divided into proximate (or immediate) and remote (or mediate). The cooperation of the merchant who supplies scalpels to an abortionist is material and proximate; the cooperation of the man who sweeps the abortionist's floor is material and remote. But I will not be using this terminology here.

The term "material" has sometimes been explained in terms of physical matter; thus, a janitor who opens a locked door for a thief is said to cooperate materially because he only makes it possible physically for the thief to do that which he has come to do; he does not actually do anything that would have to be understood as part of the primary agent's act of stealing. But this way of making the distinction can be misleading. The barrier that serves as a buffer between the formal and the material has more to do with the intelligibility of the act performed than with physicality. We see this in the janitor example. Opening a locked door, even that locked door, is probably something the janitor does every day and for various people. It makes sense—has intelligibility—on its own; when one sees a janitor opening a door for another person, one does not say to oneself, "a theft!" But if someone were to see the janitor craning his neck around the corner to see how close a policeman is and at the same time signaling to someone loading goods into a car to work faster, the person might reasonably conclude that he is witnessing a theft. And indeed he is, presuming it is a theft, even if it is not the janitor who is, strictly speaking, stealing the goods. He is just cooperating, almost certainly formally; presumably, once the thief has driven off, he will be left holding none of the goods.

A convenient way of drawing the crucial distinction is to attend to whether the cooperator wants the project of the primary agent to go forward or the *act* he performs "wants" that project to go forward. Acts falling into these two categories would involve formal cooperation; all other cooperation is material.[5] How a cooperator might want a project to go forward is pretty obvious: a legislator who introduces a less restrictive abortion law or a journalist who writes an article promoting such legislation cooperates formally in the evil of abor-

5. Some classical moralists such as Nicola Cretoni would say that, whenever a cooperator is forced against his will to cooperate, the cooperation is material. Thus, even the act of serving as lookout could be material cooperation. But it would be *at the least* immediate material cooperation—which is always immoral.

tion. But the idea of an act's wanting a project to go forward requires a bit of explaining. Obviously the "wanting" (or the intending) that attaches to a human action and causes it to be a human action comes ultimately from the cooperator himself; but the type of action he performs can already have an intelligibility that heads toward (has as its object) something evil.[6] Thus, it is possible for a man to perform an action by its own nature aimed at a project's success, even while (all things considered) he does not want to perform it. In either case— that is, in the case of a person's genuinely wanting the project to go forward and in the case of a person's not wanting to perform an action but performing it nonetheless—there is a connection between the evil deed of the primary agent and the will of the person cooperating.

Consider a person who is basically opposed to abortion, but for familial or financial reasons finds himself having to raise funds for an abortion agency. This person cooperates formally, since his fundraising activities make no sense independently of the abortionists' intention to kill. Even if he is forced to do what he does, in some sense he wants the abortion agency to succeed. His fundraising activities have sense *as* raising money for that enterprise: they are not a series of random events that happen to finish with money in the bank account of the abortionists. And now consider another case, this one taken from real life. In Germany, in order for a woman to obtain an abortion, she has to present to the abortionist a certificate testifying that she has been counseled regarding the medical facts of abortion, her various alternatives, etc. For some years the Catholic Church in Germany operated counseling centers in which such counseling was done, at the completion of which the woman was given the certificate. Doubtless, many counselors who were personally opposed to abortion signed certificates and gave them to women, knowing full well that they were handing them what they needed and wanted in

---

6. On the exterior act, see *ST* 1-2.18.6c and 1-2.20.

order to get an abortion. But because that *type* of action makes sense independently of abortion—it makes sense, that is, at the end of a counseling session to hand over a certificate saying that the counseling has taken place—the counselors cooperated, but only materially. Their cooperation was quite different from the reluctant fundraiser, since even their *acts* did not "want" the abortions to be performed.

None of this is to say, however, that the practice of issuing the certificates to women completing the counseling was a good thing—and, in fact, at the behest of John Paul II, the German bishops halted the practice. The problem, however, was not that the counselors were necessarily cooperating formally in evil, but that even any material cooperation in evil ought to be avoided *if* it might give others the impression that the cooperator does not object to the evil acts performed by the other agent or agents. Or, to use the technical phrase, material cooperation is moral only if it does not "create scandal." This is the point of John Paul II's saying, in the quotation from *Evangelium vitae* given above, that a legislator can vote for a more restrictive abortion law provided that his "absolute personal opposition to procured abortion [is] well known." In such a case a claim of personal opposition is plausible, especially assuming that the legislation is more restrictive than the previous legislation; but, in the case of the German certificates, continuing the practice posed the inevitable and inherent danger of giving the impression that the church did not genuinely believe that abortion is the immoral taking of human life. It is much more difficult—if not impossible—for an institution in such a situation to give assurances that would prevent scandal, since the point of such assurances is to establish distance between the agent and the action he is performing; but in this case the action in question is (or would be) a regular procedure of the institution itself.

Of course, it is also possible for a counselor in a Catholic agency to sign and hand over a certificate, *wanting* by that very action to facilitate an abortion. In this case, the counselor does not cooperate materially, but formally, since his intention is mixed up with the evil action. Should any person refuse to make efforts to prevent scandal caused by his cooperation in whatever evil, or should he be unconcerned that the institution for which he works or that he represents might be creating scandal, this would be *prima facie* evidence that his cooperation is not material, but rather formal, for (as it would seem) his intention is mixed up in the evil to be performed. As we saw in chapter 2, the character of an act can change depending on the circumstances that attach to it, which include the intention with which it is performed. This is not to say, however, that, when what would otherwise be material cooperation is actually formal, the badness of giving scandal is added *onto* the independently good material cooperation: the material and the formal cooperation become a single thing—a single act.

It should be fairly clear at this point why a legislator's voting for a more restrictive abortion law is not necessarily immoral. It is at most material cooperation in the evil of abortion, since the legislator's intention is not mixed up with the intention of those who perform the abortions.[7] Indeed it may be more accurate to say that such voting is not cooperation at all. Although the law in question authorizes some abortions and the legislator votes for that law (we might even say that he votes "for" that authorization), his act has sense—intelligibility—in itself; and it is clear that this intelligibility is that of an act performed so that the law will be changed to make abortion more extensively prohibited and thus less frequent. On the other hand, when a legislator votes for a less restrictive abortion law, even though an act of voting for a law that allows abortion can sometimes be moral, in this case the voting is immoral because it is formal cooperation in the evil of abortion.

7. Of course, it would be possible to imagine a case in which a legislator votes for a more restrictive law even while his intention is mixed up with the intention of abortionists. He may, for instance, have a financial interest in some abortion clinic explicitly favored by the legislation. But, for the purposes of the present investigation, we can safely ignore such cases.

Let us move on now to another, even hotter public issue in contemporary pluralistic democracies: whether to recognize homosexual marriage. This and related issues have become of such pivotal significance in the last few decades that in July 1992 the Congregation for the Doctrine of the Faith felt obliged to issue a document entitled, "Some Considerations Concerning the Response to Legislative Proposals on the Non-discrimination of Homosexual Persons," and in July 2003 another entitled, "Considerations Regarding Proposals to Give Legal Recognition to Unions Between Homosexual Persons." Obviously, there are other issues that we might have taken up, but this one is useful because of its topicality and because it clearly admits of analysis in terms of the principles articulated in the present book.

For reasons set out especially in chapter 3, it should be clear that homosexual marriage cannot be a good thing, for it goes against natural law. All of sexual morality looks to the conjugal act, which is the standard of all reasonable—and therefore moral—sexual activity. When sexual activity occurs within the context of marriage and in such a way that the integrity of the conjugal act is not violated, it is a source of wholeness and peace—not to mention (if God so grants) the occasional child. It is because of its positive goodness and benefit to society that legislators have often encouraged and protected marriage and the family by means of tax breaks and other incentives. Homosexual marriage deserves no such special consideration since, in itself, it is not a good thing; it can no sooner become a reputable institution than can lying or fraud.

What does this mean for the contemporary legislator? It means that he cannot promote the recognition of homosexual marriage, nor even the granting of a privileged status approximating that of genuine marriage to homosexual unions, since that would be to pick out and promote actions contrary to natural law. To do this would be to cooperate formally in evil, since the legislator's intentions would be mixed up with the intentions of those who engage (and/or will engage) in homosexual activity. Of course, theoretically, a legislator can vote for a law that recognizes homosexual marriage, as long as that law will, in his judgment, have the effect of reducing the number of such unions and as long as his opposition to the recognition of such unions is well known; but, given the contemporary political situation, where all the pressure is to *introduce* homosexual marriage, legislators are unlikely to be presented with a law having to do with homosexual marriage that they could vote for morally.

A person might ask: Hasn't the law already in effect acknowledged that homosexual *activity* is acceptable behavior in our democratic society? It is no longer prosecuted; few legislators today, even if they believe that homosexual acts are immoral, would be willing to sponsor legislation outlawing such acts.[8] Should we not just extend the same tolerance to homosexual unions? After all, Thomas Aquinas himself says that the issuing of unenforceable decrees can cause contempt for the law and ought sometimes to be foregone.[9] Homosexual acts seem today to have slipped below the threshold of enforceable contrary law; soon homosexual unions will do the same. So, why not just acknowledge this and concentrate on battles that can be won?

There are a number of responses one could make to this objection. In the first place, although Aquinas does say that legal prohibition of the unenforceable leads to contempt for the law and even that a society's lack of virtue contributes to the reasons not to prohibit certain vices, he specifies in the same place [*ST* 1-2.96.2] that the latter "allowable vices" do not include those that cause harm to others. Granted—but not conceded—that homosexual activity engaged in privately by consenting adults harms no "other," the recognition of homosexual marriage causes harm to those who are led to regard such a relationship as a path toward human fulfillment. The law's function is not just to permit and to prohibit, but also to instruct; and

8. In the United States, one might add that the Supreme Court has invalidated all such state legislation: see *Lawrence v. Texas* [539 U.S. 558 (2003)].

9. See *ST* 1-2.96.2, especially the reply to the second objection.

the instruction it offers can sometimes be corrupting. A legislator is obliged to do what he can to prevent such corruption.

Second, although it is conceivable that eventually homosexual marriage will become so entrenched in (at least) Western culture that a legislator might not have to decide whether to support it or oppose it (simply because no laws posing this question come before him), this has not happened yet. At the moment many legislators *are* faced with laws concerning homosexual marriage—whether it should be recognized or further recognized—and it is clear that they cannot vote in favor without cooperating in evil.

But let us assume that in some political entity a law has been passed recognizing and institutionalizing homosexual marriage. To what extent might a Christian cooperate with such a law, cooperate with such an institution? Does the immorality of homosexual marriage mean that no cooperation of any sort is permissible? Well, some actions connected with homosexual marriage get their very sense from that immoral practice; others do not. If some political entity were to insist that no person with the authority to perform marriages can refuse the request of homosexuals to marry them, such a person would be obliged to disobey the law, since performing such an action would be formal cooperation in evil.[10] It makes no difference that he would prefer not to perform such a ceremony; given the nature of the act, performing it would clearly be formal cooperation. But a worker who sets up chairs for such ceremonies might be cooperating only materially. A bailiff or clerk in a courthouse required to register such ceremonies (but not to perform them) would come closer to cooperating formally; but, here again, what such a person does has sense independently of the immoral practice. He is simply keeping a record of what goes on in the courthouse, and that makes

---

10. I presume here that the person with the authority to marry cannot morally simply cease to exercise his capacity to marry legally. This would be the situation, for instance, of a pastor or parish priest who is obliged to perform the marriages of parishioners.

sense whether the event recorded is a homosexual marriage or some other legal proceeding. Such actions can be considered material cooperation, and possibly moral, provided that scandal is not given.

Let me conclude with a very brief word about Thomas Aquinas's position regarding the duties of judges, for this will allow us to see how he would draw the line between material and formal cooperation. At one point he considers the question of whether a judge who knows the truth can issue a judgment against the truth. Aquinas maintains that a judge judges *as* a public official and so, within that context, he must use knowledge that he has as a public official, not knowledge that he has just as a private person [*ST* 2-2.67.2]. Thus, it could very well happen that a judge knows something that would exonerate a person, but has not come out in court by way of documents, witnesses, etc. He may, for instance, know that key witnesses against a man accused of a capital crime are lying. After making every legal effort to bring the truth out in court and, that having proved futile, having attempted unsuccessfully to send the case to a higher court or higher official, a judge might be obliged to sentence the accused to death—even though he knows he is innocent. But it is not he who kills the innocent man, says Aquinas, but those who testified falsely against him [*ST* 2-2.64.6 ad 3].[11]

Obviously, this judge is cooperating in evil; and clearly Aquinas believes that the cooperation is just material (although he never employs such language). The distinction he recognizes cannot be drawn in terms of physical matter, for the judge's cooperation consists in his issuing a judgment—which is to say that it depends on the independent intelligibility of what he does. The judge's intention is insulated from the evil intention—it is not mixed in with it—by virtue of the integral unity of his own job as judge. To employ the language employed above, neither he nor his act "wants" the unjust execution to

---

11. One notes that Aquinas makes this remark in the article immediately preceding the article on whether it is licit to kill in self-defense.

ensue. What he has done, as tragic as it is, makes sense independently of the unjust killing of the innocent man.

There are orthodox Catholic ethicists who do not go along with Aquinas in this regard, often arguing that a judge can, on the basis of equity (or *epieikeia*), refuse to sentence the innocent man; but these ethicists fail to acknowledge that Aquinas clearly holds that the judge can proceed to sentencing only after all other avenues have been explored and found inadequate. If on the basis of equity, legally applied, the sentencing might be stopped, Aquinas too would agree that it ought not to go forward.

The example of the judge condemning an innocent man on the basis of evidence he knows to be false (but legally irrefutable) is more useful as an indication of how Aquinas understands human action and cooperation than as a practical piece of jurisprudence. In modern legal systems, those persons responsible as jurors or magistrates for finding criminal guilt are not as rigidly constrained as judges in Aquinas's day by rules about the force and weight of admissible evidence. Moreover, there are usually available to judges various grounds on which they might recuse themselves, or declare a mistrial, even after a trial has begun.

Distinctions such as those drawn by Aquinas in discussing this question are more likely to be relevant to appellate judges called upon to review sentences of a kind provided for by law but condemned (in the relevant circumstances) by Catholic social or moral teaching: capital punishment, for instance. If they dismiss such an appeal for clemency on the grounds that there was no relevant error in law or legal procedure, thus allowing the sentence to stand or even reaffirming it, they are not mixing their intention with that of those legislators or prosecutors or jurors who intend (or intended) that such executions be carried out.

six

THE SUPREMACY OF CONSCIENCE

We come now to the issue of conscience. The English word "conscience" comes from the Latin word *conscientia,* whose central meaning is simply consciousness or knowledge. As we shall see in this chapter, this connection with knowledge is the key to understanding conscience. In Thomas Aquinas, conscience has to do both with our knowledge of general moral precepts and with their *application* in particular instances. The sphere of general precepts itself has two levels. The first is that of *synderesis,* our grasping or "having" of the first precepts of the moral life, such as that "one ought to do good and avoid evil" and that "the precepts of God ought to be obeyed." Every human being who is not deprived of free will (by, for instance, injury or disease) has *synderesis* and therefore knows that good is to be done, evil avoided, and the precepts of God obeyed. The second level within the sphere of general precepts is the sphere of reason. At this level a man can err. Although he never ceases to know that good is to be done, he may think that good can be done by, for instance, committing adultery. (This is an example used frequently by Aquinas.)

In contemporary language the word "conscience" has come to signify not so much the application of general precepts in particular instances as one's practical and habitual comprehension of the general precepts, of which one is made especially aware when going against it.[1] The two senses, however, are closely related. One has qualms of conscience with respect to actions (applications) in tension with general precepts, with the result that one is made aware of the inclinations (the practical and habitual comprehension) associated with those general precepts. In the present chapter I employ both senses of conscience; the context in which I use the word should make clear which sense I am employing.[2]

A good entrance into the issue of conscience is a problem raised by Plato and, to an extent, resolved by Aristotle. That a consideration of conscience should begin in ancient philosophy ought not to sur-

1. In classical Catholic moral theology the first sense—application—is often referred to as "actual conscience," the second—comprehension—as "habitual conscience."

2. In a work in which he is arguing that the doctrine of papal infallibility does not impede full participation in democratic society, John Henry Newman writes, "conscience is not a judgment upon any speculative truth, any abstract doctrine, but bears on something to be done or not done. 'Conscience,' says St. Thomas, 'is the practical judgment or dictate of reason, by which we judge what *hic et nunc* is to be done as being good, or to be avoided as evil.' Hence conscience cannot come into direct collision with the church's or the Pope's infallibility, which is engaged on general propositions, and in the condemnation of particular and given errors"; Newman, "A Letter Addressed to His Grace the Duke of Norfolk on Occasion of Mr. Gladstone's Recent Expostulation," in *Certain Difficulties Felt by Anglicans in Catholic Teaching Considered*, 2:256. As John Finnis has pointed out, the quotation is not from Aquinas, but from St. Alphonsus Liguori. More importantly, Finnis argues against Newman's general thesis, as follows: "Newman's discourse at this point has shifted, without warning, from the 'habitual' to the 'actual' conscience. (See previous note.) There can be no objection to that; both are legitimate senses of 'conscience' and there is no incompatibility between them. But his argument here forgets that the actual conscience, being a rational (even if mistaken) judgement about a particular option, is an *application* of rational (even if mistaken) norms and principles of judgement—at the highest level, the principles understood and affirmed in the habitual conscience." So, Finnis concludes, one's conscientious final judgment can indeed "come into direct collision" with a general proposition which has been infallibly proposed; Finnis, "Conscience in the *Letter to the Duke of Norfolk*," in *Newman After a Hundred Years*, edited by Ian Ker and Alan G. Hill (Oxford: Clarendon, 1990), 413–14.

prise us, for questions about conscience are really just questions about how far the realm of moral responsibility—which itself depends upon the agent's knowledge—extends. Plato and Aristotle were especially attentive to such fundamental issues. Aquinas's understanding of conscience is a development—or, perhaps better, a making more precise—of Aristotle's key insights in these regards.

So, what was Plato's problem? In the first book of the *Republic,* the dramatic character Socrates is conversing with a certain Cephalus as they both seek to determine the definition of justice. Cephalus, who is wealthy, says that the greatest good he has derived from his wealth is that it has allowed him peace of mind concerning his dealings with others. When the day of final reckoning arrives, he says, he will be able to say that he has cheated no one and lied to no one; without wealth, together with goodwill, he might not have been able to say this.

Socrates commends Cephalus for this remark, but then he says:

> But this itself of which you speak, justice, *ought* we to say that it is to tell the truth simply speaking in this way and to make return should someone receive something from another? Or are not even these things sometimes done justly, sometimes unjustly? I mean the following. If a man receives arms from a friend who is of sound mind and if this friend, having gone out of his mind, should ask for their return, would not everyone say that it is not necessary to return them—the one returning such things would *not* be just—nor is it necessary willingly to tell the truth to someone in such a state? [331C1–8; see also ii.382C7–D4.]

The question here is basically whether we can make a connection between general precepts, such as "return things loaned to you" or "deal truthfully with others," and the particular cases where the same precepts may or may not apply. Socrates' (that is, Plato's) answer is that, no, the general precepts cannot reach down into concrete particularity in that way; the only reliable moral knowledge we have is knowledge of the precepts, which are part of the idea of justice, whose place in the universe is separate from particular actions such as one's returning (or failing to return) things given to one in trust.

Aristotle's response to this was to recognize two types of intellectual activity: theoretical reasoning and practical reasoning. In theoretical reasoning, the basic pattern of thought is the syllogism, as in "All men are rational animals; all Greeks are men; therefore, all Greeks are rational animals." This can be described as top-down reasoning and (roughly) Platonic: one begins with two premises and *from* these deduces the conclusion. There is nothing in the conclusion that is not pulled down from the premises. Practical reasoning might be thought of as proceeding in the opposite direction. It is also true that here one often begins with an end, then considers various ways of getting to that end, and, finally, performs an action. This too can be described as top-down reasoning. But the practical realm is not primarily concerned with such reasoning *about* what to do, but about doing it. Placing the emphasis on action, practical reasoning can be conceived of as starting from an action (referred to by Aristotle as a conclusion), going up through whatever intermediate steps are deemed necessary, until one gets up *to* the end.

In this process, one is not pulling the contents of the conclusion (the action) out of the things higher up (the intermediate steps and the end): the action is a concrete particular in its own right, not deduced from those other things. One sees this same sort of thing throughout the practical realm. One of the higher precepts of the natural law is "Respect one's neighbor." Closely related to this, *almost* as if conclusions drawn from premises, are a society's laws regarding real estate boundaries. These laws will inevitably involve provisions appropriate to the particular place where they have effect. In rugged, scarcely populated terrain, boundaries might be only approximate; in a city, they will be very precise indeed and may even include vertical limits—so-called "sky rights." None of these particularities is contained *in* the precept "Respect one's neighbor." The particular real estate laws are ways of getting to—or acting in accordance with—the precept "Respect one's neighbor," given certain (in this case quite literally) mundane facts about the situation in which one acts.

This approach allows Aristotle to solve Plato's problem, although—it must be acknowledged—he does not actually formulate such a solution. Aquinas, however, does. Following Aristotle's general approach (and reliant upon Aristotle's knowledge of Plato), Aquinas explicitly discusses the question of whether one should always return deposits, such as the arms received from a friend as mentioned in Plato's *Republic* [*ST* 1-2.94.4]. His answer is no, since what we might call "the deposits precept" is more distant from the highest precepts of the natural law than are other precepts. An example of a precept closer to the highest precepts would be "Do not lie," which allows of no exceptions.

But is this not, someone might argue, to adopt a Platonic approach at least with respect to precepts of the same rank as the deposits precept? The answer is again, no, for practical reason is in the first instance about acts. If in every situation lying is incompatible with the higher precepts at which, in accordance with human nature, we aim, it is thus because there is something unintelligible and therefore wrong about any particular lie, even if there is a good reason to tell it. But there is nothing unintelligible or wrong about not returning a weapon to a mad depositor: nothing at all. The moral universe is simply made up of precepts of different ranks such as these.

In his *Disputed Questions on Truth,* Thomas considers the question, "Does conscience bind?"[3] His answer is that, yes, it does, but that the way in which it binds is only analogously related to the way in which binding occurs in the physical world. In speaking of binding in the physical world, Thomas has in mind the influence that a physical object might have upon another so that the one compels or obliges the other to move. Whereas in physical movement for such a bond to be effective there must be physical contact between the the two

---

3. Aquinas, "Utrum conscientia liget"; *Quaestiones disputatate de veritate* 17.3. For this work, I use the abbreviation *QD de ver.*

objects, no such contact is necessary for conscience to bind: it becomes binding through knowledge.

If, for instance, a man knows that adultery is wrong but, through no fault of his own, does not know that the woman in his bed is not his wife, his conscience telling him never to commit adultery does not establish a bond or link with the act that he is about to perform (intercourse with the woman in his bed). If he performs the act, he is not guilty of adultery. If, on the other hand, he does know that she is not his wife, he is obviously bound by his conscience not to have intercourse with her—which is to say (in Thomistic terms) that *synderesis* and reason have a morally significant bearing upon the action performed. Citing Aristotle's *Metaphysics* [v.1.1013a10–14], Thomas compares this type of binding to the way in which citizens are bound by the decision of a king or governor. Required here is not physical contact between the king or governor and his subjects, but simply their knowledge that the king or governor has chosen to promulgate a law or decree. A subject's violating a law of which he has knowledge (and by which he is therefore obliged) does not, of course, cause the bond to disappear—that would only happen if knowledge was absent—but it does put the bond under strain. A large part of morality is the avoidance of such strain, for it points to a lack of unity within the soul—and ultimately to a lack of unity or intelligibility within the corresponding society.

The fact that we typically immediately pick up the link between our particular actions and general precepts, as understood by *synderesis* and reason, is a good indication that there is something wrong with Plato's approach. Determining whether something is a moral thing to do or to have done is very rarely a matter of beginning with a general rule ("return things given to you in trust") and *trying*—sometimes unsuccessfully—to apply it to a particular case. It is usually a matter rather of a person's knowing immediately and full well what he is doing and his being made aware, by that familiar and characteristic visceral tensing, that this cannot be a sound application of his own higher precepts.

An idea fundamental to any Aristotelian theory, of ethics or whatever, is the idea that inconsistency is not a good thing. In ethics, inconsistency usually manifests itself in strain upon the bond that is, especially clearly in Thomas, conscience. As already stated, such inconsistency does not mean that the bond of conscience is broken, but only that reason, standing under *synderesis*, has not been properly applied. We perform acts in order to get things or to achieve certain states. Those things or those states are only attractive insofar as they fall under the end toward which a person is headed—that is, the good as he conceives it. This end is the concern of *synderesis* ("one ought to do good and avoid evil"). If there is *no* such link, no bond, between a particular action and the final end, that action is not a human action at all, but something standing outside of ethics altogether, like the involuntary kick that comes of a doctor's tapping one's knee with a rubber mallet. But, once this bond is present, it is a bad thing to put strain upon it, for strain is a tendency toward breaking apart: a tendency toward the unintelligible, and therefore the irrational or nonhuman.

One experiences moral strain in a number of ways. It often follows an instance of knowing what one ought to do and not doing it. In the classical literature, this is called (is an instance of) weakness of will, or *akrasia.* Since no one can ever extinguish *synderesis,* but only deflect it in such a way that one does not apply its dictates,[4] the weak-willed man experiences strain in an obvious way: one part of his soul calls him in the right direction (to do good), another leads him to perform an act incompatible with that call. It is apparent here how conscience is binding: the person *ought* to have applied his higher precepts in a different way by performing a different act or by not performing any act. Such a person typically experiences remorse after the event, which is a signal that unity of soul has been compromised to some extent. This bond is dependent upon knowledge: knowledge

4. *QD de ver.* 16.3c.

of what the ruling part of the soul demands and of what one is doing. From this knowledge emerges the sting of remorse.

Another case would be the following. Suppose a man decides at some point that doing the right thing will simply not get him what he wants; he chooses, therefore, in a maybe more, maybe less explicit manner, to make the general object of his life the gratification of a particular disordered desire, such as the desire to dominate others. Reason is still present in this man telling him that what he does is not good or right, but he pushes it away from consideration. Aristotle calls this "ignorance by choice."[5] Since this man never says to himself—in any case, with any conviction—that what he does is actually the right thing to do, in *this* sense he is not unlike the former (weak-willed) man, for his acts do not correspond to what reason tells him he should be doing. The bond of conscience in his soul is strained, since he knows that he is not following the dictate of *synderesis* to do good and to avoid evil. The difference between him and the weak-willed man is that he has successfully pushed reason (attached to *synderesis*) into the background of his life and lives primarily in the realm of application. He probably regards himself as a hands-on kind of guy. As a result, what he feels as a consequence of his actions is not, strictly speaking, remorse, for he has previously ceased to orient his life toward the good; the effect of his more ingrained inconsistency is rather a sort of dull emptiness.

Yet another case would be that of the man who quite deliberately performs actions inconsistent with objective morality, but who (unlike the man in the previous paragraph) believes that what he does *is* pursuing the good and avoiding evil. In this man there is agreement between his general commitment to pursuing the good and avoiding evil and the behavior that he believes to be correct behavior. But his more general demeanor, including his adhering to the erroneous position regarding the character of his actions, is inconsistent with

5. Aristotle, *EN* iii.1.1110b31–32.

objective morality, which depends upon reason and upon the same general precepts also known by him through *synderesis*. This ethical type can be divided into two subtypes: the man whose erroneous ideas about the good are his own fault, and the man whose erroneous ideas are not his own fault. Both men will experience strain of some sort, although (as I shall argue), strictly speaking, the strain experienced by the latter is not strain upon the bond of *conscience*.

According to Thomas, any man with an erroneous conscience, whether culpable or not, is bound to follow it. He is obliged to do this because his erroneous conscience is still a bond, which is simply to say that there is an intelligible connection between this man's higher precepts—including, especially, the precept that "one ought to do good and avoid evil"—and their application in particular acts. Not to perform an act believed obligatory (or to fail to avoid an act believed prohibited) would put strain on this bond—and strain, as we have seen, is not a good thing. But, although the man with the erroneous conscience is obliged to follow his conscience, if he might have avoided the false understanding he has acquired, he still commits evil in doing what he believes is the right thing to do (*ST* 1-2.19.6c)—that is, in performing that particular act.

This theory strikes some people as strange or even as itself inconsistent. But it is no more strange or inconsistent than any assertion of a necessary, but nonsufficient condition for behaving morally. The theory simply says that *one* condition of behaving morally is that you do what you believe is right, although this does not necessarily settle the question of whether the behavior itself is moral. One must also make sure that the action performed *is* a good action (and not a bad action), if such knowledge is at all possible. Similarly, telling the truth is in itself a good thing to do, although this does not settle the question of whether a particular act of truth-telling is moral. When, for instance, a person tells someone the truth with the intention of driving him to suicide, telling the truth remains in itself a good thing to do, although that act of telling the truth is immoral. We find a similar thing in the case of the binding erroneous conscience. This binding is a central—but not the sole—issue.

An objection that takes us to the heart of the general theory might go as follows. (We considered it also briefly in chapter 2.) For something to be immoral, it must enter into the realm of human action, and for this to happen, the agent must know what he is doing—that is, he must know that what he is doing is immoral. If a person does not believe that an act is immoral, he obviously does not *know* that it is immoral; so how can it be that a person does wrong in following his erroneous conscience? One way of meeting this challenge would be simply to cite authority and, in particular, the authority of Aristotle. Aristotle maintains that there are three ways—and only three ways—in which a particular action (or an aspect of an action) might be taken out of the realm of culpability. The first is force, as when one's hand is forced to trace out one's name on a document. The second is ignorance of particular circumstances, such as that the woman in bed is not one's wife. The third is more universal ignorance, for which the person acting is in no way responsible.[6] Since there are just these three ways in which an act (or an aspect of an act) might be nonculpable and since the acts we are considering correspond to none of them, one who performs such an act is culpable for the evil in the act performed, and not just for the ignorance.

Obviously, however, an argument from authority will not satisfy the objector who insists that, when there is no bond of conscience or knowledge between an agent and his act, he cannot be blamed for committing the evil that someone else might recognize in the act. But we can supply an argument in Aristotle's and Thomas's support. It is true that ignorance of a particular act's immorality eliminates

6. This type of universal exonerating ignorance is implicit at *EN* iii.1.1110b32–33, where a *certain* type of universal ignorance is said to deserve flogging. Elsewhere Aristotle specifies that this ignorance presupposes negligence: "someone not having [knowledge of what he should do] might be blamed if, because of carelessness or pleasure or pain, he does not have what it is easy or necessary to have"; *EE* ii.9.1225b14–16. Universal ignorance due neither to carelessness, pleasure, or pain is not culpable.

the possibility of a bond of conscience with respect to the particular act in question and, therefore, the possibility of a strain upon such a bond, but it does not exclude conscience from consideration altogether, nor does it exclude knowledge pertaining to the act sufficient to declare this agent's performance of the act immoral.

Consider a stockbroker who is willfully ignorant of the fact that a particular type of negotiation constitutes insider trading. (In fact, the legal principles pertaining to insider trading are complicated and the corresponding laws sometimes counterintuitive.) Since the stock market is his trade, the stockbroker is obliged to know the relevant law. He would rather *not* know it, however, and so on a particular occasion he does not know that the act he performs is illegal (and immoral), although he knows that it could be. In this case, his conscience is indeed clear with respect to the particular action—there is consistency between his understanding of the ethics of the stock market and that particular stock negotiation—but his conscience also tells him, or would have told him in the past, that he ought to know what the law says about whatever stock negotiations he might be involved in. This bond of conscience is distinct from his bond of conscience with respect to the particular stock negotiation, but it does bring in, by another route, knowledge (and therefore also *synderesis*) having a bearing upon that action. This knowledge is tenuous—he knows only that the law of which he is culpably ignorant *could* have a bearing upon his action—but that is enough to bring culpability to that particular act. It will possibly also bring a tug of conscience with respect to that particular action.

In other words, the bond of conscience between the stockbroker's understanding of the law and this particular stock negotiation may not be under strain that can be associated with knowledge of the law and its particular application, but the stockbroker is aware of his ignorance of the law. He may have made the choice not to bother about the law long ago, but that is still part of his character and background knowledge. He also knows that his past decisions (and his ignorance) have a bearing upon the particular things he does as a stockbroker. Since the man knows that any negotiations fall under the law in a way that is morally significant (although he does not *know* that this one is immoral), the particular action at issue falls under the general precept that "one ought to do good and avoid evil"—that is to say, under *synderesis*. It is this that ultimately accounts for tugs of conscience, if and when they arrive.

The law presumes this sort of analysis. The willfully ignorant stockbroker who engages even unknowingly in insider trading is guilty of *insider trading* and not just of ignorance, since the law, which he is obliged to know, is about particular stock negotiations. An indication that there does exist a bond between the law, whether known or not, and the particular negotiation is the fact that, if it turns out that the stock negotiation was *not* illegal (the stockbroker being ignorant also of this), the stockbroker's action would not be culpable—although he may still be morally culpable for his failure to know the law. This change of fate for the stockbroker would occur because of what is in the law regarding that particular type of action. Had that particular negotiation been illegal, he would be going to jail.

Thomas takes just such an approach in *ST* 1-2.19.6, where he discusses an erroneous conscience regarding adultery. His point is that, even if one's conscience is clear when performing the immoral act, one's will, which gathers together all one's bonds of conscience, is not right, since one either willed not to know that one ought not to perform such an action or one was negligent in this regard (for negligence, too, is a state of the will). Similarly, to recall *Disputed Questions on Truth* (17.3), if a king or governor posts a decree in the appropriate place in the town square but, out of contempt for him or simply out of negligence, one of his subjects typically avoids that part of the town square, if the subject violates the decree, he does so culpably, since his will is not right and that will has a bearing upon the particular acts he performs.

Even in the case of a nonculpably erroneous conscience a lack of consistency is involved, although here it does not pertain to the person's conscience in the strict sense. The inconsistency is present by virtue of the fact that what the person believes he should do (and in fact does) is inconsistent with the moral law. Imagine a young man brought up in an isolated primitive society where sleeping with one's brother's wife is considered moral and where, because of the isolation, it would have been utterly impossible for him to come to understand that this custom is immoral. (To this end, we might also suppose that he is of very low intelligence.) In such a case, there would be inconsistency between the young man's beliefs and the moral truth that adultery is always wrong, although his act of sleeping with his brother's wife would not be culpable, for his will has not been involved in his failure to know that such acts are immoral.

The only reason someone might have for saying that even this case involves strain upon conscience is the fact that the precept forbidding adultery follows closely upon other precepts that the young man supposedly does grasp, including the general precept "one ought to do good and avoid evil." A person's general sense of what is fair and truthful, what is healthy for social relationships and what is not, would be enough (or so the argument goes) to generate the tension characteristic of a bad conscience. But it is quite possible to know the premises of a syllogism without knowing the conclusion—and, as we have already seen, here we are not even dealing with deduction in the strict sense, such as that which takes place when one draws a conclusion from a syllogism. The young man does not know the quasi-conclusion prohibiting adultery. Since conscience depends on knowledge, whatever he might sense is not the tug of conscience. It is similar rather to the dull emptiness of the man spoken of above who is ignorant by choice, except that in this case the young man is not responsible for the ignorance. What he quite possibly feels is simply a lack of human fulfillment.

What does all this mean for our approach to people's responsibility for their actions? In the first place, it means that there is theoretical space to exonerate *some* people for the bad actions they perform in good faith. In *ST* 1-2.19.6, having said in the previous article that an erroneous conscience binds, Thomas says that, "if erring reasoning should say that a man is obliged to have intercourse with the wife of another, the will agreeing with this reasoning is evil because this error is due to ignorance of the law of God, which one is obliged to know." I suppose here that Thomas would agree that the young man growing up in primitive isolation would be an exception to this rule, especially if we add that low intelligence is also a factor in his not knowing (see *Disputed Questions on Truth* 16.3c); but Thomas's bluntness with respect to adultery is indication that claims of inculpably erroneous conscience are generally sustainable only when the precept in question stands at some distance from the highest moral precepts. The example that Thomas gives of a more sustainable claim is that of certain heretics who maintain that all oaths are immoral, when in fact some oaths—those taken in court to "tell the truth and nothing but the truth," for example—are not.[7]

This rule against oath taking is not unlike the deposits precept of Platonic origin, considered above—that is, the precept "return things loaned to you." It is imaginable that a person might take this rule so seriously that, when confronted by the argument "If you do not return the arms to me, you are breaking the law," he would feel obliged to make the return. If a person has not had the opportunity to study ethical theory and so to learn that certain (but not all) general rules might fail in their application—or if a person has not had the opportunity to study law and so to learn that the law itself allows exceptions to the general dictum "return things loaned to you"—he might return the arms, thereby performing an act that is, objectively speaking, wrong, but do so nonculpably.

---

7. *QD de ver.* 17.2c. The Leonine edition of *QD de ver.,* citing sources, mentions Manichaeans and Waldensians as having held that all oaths are prohibited by God; *Quaestiones disputatae de veritate:* QQ.13–20 (Rome: Commissio Leonina, 1972); *Opera Omnia,* vol. 22.2, fasc. 2, 520, note to line 88.

With respect to positions like those of the heretics who insist that all oath-taking is immoral, Thomas would certainly follow the legal tradition already established in his day that those who hold heretical positions but do so without "pertinacious animosity" ought not to be regarded as heretics [*ST* 2-2.11.2 ad 3]. That tradition gave as a possible reason for such lack of animosity the passing on of religious convictions from one generation to the next. The progeny may never have had occasion to doubt or to investigate these convictions.[8] It is considerations such as these that have allowed the church in more recent years to speak more positively of the separated ecclesial communities and to speak, as part of its effort to promote ecumenical dialogue, of the Christian riches to be discovered in them. Says the Vatican II decree *Unitatis redintegratio,* "The children who are born into these communities and who grow up believing in Christ cannot be accused of the sin involved in the separation, and the Catholic Church embraces them as brothers, with respect and affection" [§3]. The church is thereby respecting the bond of conscience of people who grow up in such traditions and exonerating at least some of them on the grounds that their ignorance of the full truth is not due to choice or to negligence. Of course, if a man comes to comprehend the more complete truth and performs actions incompatible with it,

---

8. The position comes ultimately from Augustine's 43rd letter, where he writes: "But those who defend their own opinion, even if it be false and perverse, if they do so without pertinacious animosity—especially if it is an opinion they have acquired not by their own presumption but from parents who have been deceived and fallen into error—and who, prepared to be corrected, seek the truth with careful solicitude, these individuals, when they are encountered, ought never to be regarded as heretics"; Jacques-Paul Migne, ed., *Patrologiae cursus completes,* Series Latina (Paris: Imprimerie Catholique, 1844–1864), vol. 33, col. 160. In *ST* 2-2.11.2 ad 3, Thomas leaves out the interjected phrase about parents who have fallen into error because he is explaining how doctors of the church such as Jerome and Augustine can without culpability disagree on issues pertaining to the faith (such as the cessation of legal decrees put forward in the Old Testament). Their disagreement had nothing to do with a heretical upbringing. Augustine's remark found its way into Gratian's *Decretals* (2.24.3, canon 29, "*Dixit Apostolus*").

he performs those actions culpably, and for the same reason: because he is bound to follow his conscience.

The same latitude is not available to those brought up in the Catholic tradition, and especially not to priests and religious whose education has exposed them in more depth to the teachings of the church. A Catholic priest, for instance, is not without fault if he believes that a sacramental marriage is dissoluble and acts upon that belief; a non-Catholic might be. The question is never whether such a person *agrees* with the church—we have seen that Aristotle and Thomas both assign culpability to the man who chooses not to know the truth—but whether he has *access* to the truth. And we can presume that such a person does have access to the truth, which he has either neglected or rejected outright.

seven

LIFE-AND-DEATH DECISIONS

Most of us will never have to make decisions about whether to condemn a murderer to death or to bomb a munitions factory—decisions, that is, of the type discussed previously in this book, especially in chapter 4 on the ethics of killing; but we are quite likely to be called upon to make life-and-death decisions regarding ourselves or on behalf of close relatives who cannot make their wishes known. What must be assured in all such decisions is not only that the sick, the injured, and the dying (including ourselves) be cared for as befits human dignity, but also that we who make such decisions do so in a way that is consistent with natural law. As Christians we believe that eternal life together with our loved ones in the company of saints and (especially) God is a possibility. We do not want to exclude ourselves from this future joy by making decisions here on earth incompatible with it.

A good way into a proper understanding of the morality of life-and-death decisions is a consideration of omissions of action. The way in which omissions figure into morality is anything but straightforward and, as a consequence, it is easy to become confused—or to deceive ourselves—about them. Sometimes, for instance, it is thought that omissions are so different from positive acts that one should think twice before putting a person on an artificial respirator—on the grounds perhaps that to positively withdraw such a means would be immoral, but simply to omit to employ such a means is permitted. The truth is that it can be moral to unplug a respirator and it can be immoral to omit to use one. It is sometimes thought that the omission of any means likely to prolong life is equivalent to voluntary killing. The truth is that one can sometimes omit means that would certainly prolong life and in so doing simply allow the person to die: one would not be *killing* him. Understanding omissions is useful not only because it allows us to determine which acts (or absences of acts) are moral and which immoral, but also because such an understanding gives us insight into the logic of the whole field of life-and-death decisions.

In *ST* 1-2.6.3 St. Thomas asks "whether the voluntary can be without any act." His answer is as follows:

> That which proceeds from the will is called voluntary. Now something is said to proceed from something else in two ways. One way is directly: that is, something proceeds from something else inasmuch as this other thing *acts,* as when heating proceeds from heat. Another way is indirectly: something proceeds from something else because the latter does *not* act, as when the submersion of a ship is said to proceed from the pilot, inasmuch as he leaves off piloting. (It needs to be acknowledged, however, that that which follows upon absence of action is not always reducible—by virtue of the fact that the other thing does not act—as if to an agent cause; this happens only when the other thing can and ought to act. For if a pilot *could* not direct the ship or if the piloting of the ship was not assigned to him, the submersion of the ship—which occurred for lack of a pilot—would not be blamed on him.)
>
> Because, therefore, by willing and acting the will is able—and sometimes ought—to impede not-willing and not-acting, this not-willing and not-acting is imputed to the will, as though issuing from it. And so the voluntary can be present in the absence of an act: sometimes in the absence of an exterior act but *with* an interior act,

as when someone wills not to act; sometimes also without an interior act, as when someone does not will [not to act].[1]

So, Thomas holds that a person can be held responsible for not doing something insofar as that thing's not happening can be traced back ("reduced") in some way to his will; this may or may not involve an interior act of the will immediately connected with the thing's not happening.

This latter idea is perhaps the most difficult. Thomas's approach is related to the idea we considered in chapter 6 on the supremacy of conscience, where we saw that an act can have a connection with one's will even in the absence of explicit knowledge regarding the act's morality. There I used the example of a stockbroker who is negligently ignorant of details of the law regarding insider trading. Because he is a stockbroker by profession, he is obliged to know the regulations regarding stock trading and so is culpable for individual violations of that law, even though, when he acts, he does not know that he is breaking the law. Here in *ST* 1-2.6.3, Thomas's point is that a ship's sinking can be a pilot's fault even if he never says to himself anything like, "I will not go to the helm tonight." Given that he is the ship's pilot—piloting is his profession and the ship's command has been assigned to him—his duty to be at the helm may never have occurred to him (as he dropped off to sleep, for instance) and yet he would be culpable for the ship's going down. On the other hand, a pilot who could not have been at the helm or who was not obliged to be there is not culpable; in this case, his omitting to be at the helm does not figure into the nexus of responsibility for the ship's going down.

What this shows is that the scope of responsibility in moral situations in which omissions are a factor is limited. Thomas speaks in this regard of obligations (positive obligations) that are binding "always, but not at every moment": they go hand in hand with the possibility of sinning by omission. "An omission," he says,

---

1. It appears that Thomas takes the example from Aristotle: see *Metaph.* v.2.1013b11–16; see also *Phys.* ii.3.195a12–14; in Thomas, see also *ST* 1-2.71.5c.

is opposed to an affirmative precept, which, although it obliges always, does not oblige at every moment. For a man is not obliged to remain always honoring his parents but a man *is* always obliged to honor his parents at the proper time. Therefore the sin of omission remains operative, as long as the period lasts during which the affirmative precept obliges. When that period passes, the sin ceases to be operative even while the guilt remains; when such a period resumes again, so also resumes the omission.[2]

When Thomas says here that an omission is "opposed to an affirmative precept," he does not mean that the two are unrelated: to be opposed is to "stand opposite" something as its proper contrary. Thus, an omission is the mirror image of a positive precept, and both are limited in scope. Obligations, the omissions of which are culpable, are far-extending—extending, that is, as we have seen, even to events that have no real agents; but they are also limited: limited by the scope of the positive precepts of the discipline or practice to which they pertain, so that some omissions fall outside that scope entirely. By contrast, a negative precept such as "Do not kill the innocent" is binding always and at every moment; the particular discipline or practice to which it pertains does not impose a limit upon it.

Since so many life-and-death decisions have to do with possibly culpable omissions and their corresponding positive precepts, it is apparent that determining what a good life-and-death decision is has to do with the discipline within which it is made and that discipline's precepts. This goes contrary to many contemporary approaches to moral decision-making, which tend, in our era's typically individualistic manner, to limit moral analysis to a consideration of what the individual aims at: what goes through his mind. The Aristotelian and Thomistic approach is very different: while the "perspective of

---

2. Aquinas, *De malo* 2.1 ad 11(a); see also *Sent.* 2.22.2.1 ad 4; 2.35.1.3 ad 3; also *ST* 2-2.79.3. In order to remain consistent with this language, in what follows I will refer to positive duties within a discipline such as medicine as precepts. Thus, a proper medical procedure would be a precept.

the acting person" is important and even essential, in assessing that person's action morally one must also take into consideration the precepts of the particular sector of life to which it belongs. There is a relevant field of competency proper to government, for instance, another proper to philosophy, and yet another to the family. Each such field of competency revolves around goods to be sought in a rational manner—that is, in a manner that remains within the proper obligatory scope of that discipline's particular set of positive precepts. To confuse these various fields of competency is a step toward indeterminacy—and, ultimately, chaos—in moral decision-making.

Most issues in medical ethics have to do, of course, at least indirectly with the discipline of medicine; so we must consider that discipline—that sector of life—first of all. As we saw in chapter 2, at its definitional core, medicine consists of physical acts aimed at (1) promoting or protecting the health of the bodies of the persons who are the objects of those acts and (2) removing from those bodies (as best it can) diseases and other maladies. Thus, an abortion is not a medical procedure, since it does not promote or protect, but rather destroys the health of the body that falls under the scalpel (or under the suction hose or whatever); but removing a cancerous uterus is a proper medical procedure.

A medical doctor does not violate the positive precepts of medicine when he decides truthfully that, from a medical perspective, a particular medical procedure is futile, and so omits or terminates it— even if he knows that its absence is likely to hasten death. Although length of life is certainly a factor in physical health, medicine's object is not simply to lengthen life. If that were the case, any means of extending life-duration would become obligatory, such as putting patients at a certain age into a state of frozen animation, if that is likely to stave off the moment of death.

Medicine is a helping profession in more than one sense. Obviously, its task is to help patients; but it is also a helper—and merely a helper—to that which is truly in charge in the discipline of medicine itself: nature, as manifest in the health of a human body.[3] If health is the captain of the ship, medicine is its first mate. Medicine does not *produce* health: when medicine (in the person of a doctor) arrives on duty, it finds health already up and running; if it does not, it can do nothing. Its task is to help nature to do what only *it* can do in a particular body. When, toward the end of a patient's life, a medical doctor decides legitimately (that is, on good medical grounds) not to employ a procedure and the patient dies "as a consequence," the doctor is not the cause from which the death proceeds. His job was only to stand by—and to help as much as he could—while health attempted to bring the body past whatever crisis it was facing; medicine cannot step in *for* health. Neither, of course, is the captain—health itself—to blame. He has been at his station to the end, although unsuccessfully (as inevitably happens for all of us).

What does it mean for a doctor to decide "on good medical grounds" to stand aside? Again, the image of the captain and his first mate is useful. If the captain might legitimately complain that his first mate was not at his job—that *had* he received the appropriate help from the first mate, the ship would be sailing along and on course— then the first mate (the doctor) has not decided on good medical grounds to omit to act. But one can well imagine a captain of a ship, knowing that the ship is going down, telling his first mate that his usual procedures make no sense any more ... and his being right in that assessment.

Understanding this can be a great aid to family members who must make life-and-death decisions regarding a loved one. Bringing the family into consideration at this point is not—as I have warned against—to confuse sectors of life and sets of precepts. Families too are governed by particular moral precepts, some expressed in law and some not. It is the family's responsibility to make reasonable and loving decisions about how to expend its resources—both financial

3. See Aristotle's *EN* x.4.1174b25–26.

and human—in the care of the sick and elderly. A particular family member might also have been deputed by a now-incapacitated loved one to make decisions on his behalf about whether to initiate or to omit certain medical procedures. The medical profession acts beyond its competency if it overrides such competencies as belong properly to the family. But this does not mean (by a sort of reverse parity of reasoning) that the precepts of medicine are beyond the legitimate concerns of the family. The moral competency of families and that of medicine are distinct, but they are also interrelated. A family ought not to ignore what medicine prescribes (if it says, for instance, that a lactose-intolerant child ought not to drink milk); it is also part of responsible medical practice to respect—to the extent possible and not inconsistent with medicine's ultimate goals—a patient's wishes (or those of a legitimate proxy) regarding care.

Aristotle himself speaks about these matters in the first book of the *Politics*—that is, in the very place where he insists that the various sectors and disciplines of the city must be kept distinct. (He also speaks in the passage about the competency of government, which we shall discuss shortly.) "In a sense," he says, "it is the concern of the householder and the ruler to think about health; in another sense, it is not their concern but the doctor's" [*Pol.* i.10.1258a31–32]. Thomas comments upon this remark that, "in a certain sense, it pertains to the householder or the ruler of the city to consider health, that is, in making use of the counsel of physicians for the health of its subjects; in another sense, however, it does not pertain to them, that is, the consideration of by what means health might be preserved or restored."[4] Like medical doctors, families are at the service of health (the health of their members)—although not in the technical way that the doctors are. (As Thomas says, their competency does not involve the "means" by which "health might be preserved or restored.") At a

---

4. Thomas Aquinas, *Sententia libri Politicorum* (Rome: Commissio Leonina, 1971), vol. 48 of *Opera Omnia* 1.8.197–202 (§132).

certain point a family might decide not to accept what the doctors decide, on good medical grounds, to do; or they might insist that the doctors do what they have decided, again, on good medical grounds, not to do. If following such a family directive is possible, given financial restraints, etc., and does not contradict the nature of medicine (by, for instance, abandoning hope of improved health where such hope is not unreasonable), the doctors should accede to the family's wishes.

In making such decisions, a family must be satisfied that the medical personnel caring for their loved one are as competent as possible, given the circumstances, and that they are telling the truth about their loved one's prospects and the possibilities of recovery. Once they are satisfied on these counts, they need not worry that omission or non-introduction of a medical procedure is *as such* immoral. On the other hand, as already suggested, it is also within their competency to insist with a doctor that the patient would have wanted more active intervention than is currently being provided. (Of course, the patient himself, if *compos mentis,* can insist on the same thing.) A family's responsibility for the health of its members enjoys a certain primacy over that of a doctor. In the end, doctors, *qua* doctors, are technicians; they may very well have no personal relationship at all with a patient, and they very likely know very little about his aspirations and particular capacities. The family is in quite a different position. Family members are positively obliged to love and care for one another—and, in particular, children for their parents;[5] they almost always have fuller knowledge of their loved one's aspirations and capacities. Their obligations, therefore, with respect to and in the interest of health are more direct. Respect for these obligations and consequent preferences is part of medicine, for it aims at the general well-being of the patient through caring for his physical well-being.

As mentioned, it could be that it is not the family, but the doc-

5. We might cite Ex. 20:11 and Deut. 5:15, without suggesting, however, that this obligation is not also found in natural law (see chapter 1).

tor who is against omitting (or ceasing to employ) a medical procedure. A doctor might see, for instance, that a family is not doing for
a "loved one" even that which is called for medically. He would be
acting outside his competency to insist on more effort than medicine
itself calls for; but he might legitimately ignore the wishes of a family he is convinced really wants to be rid of one of their members as
soon as possible. Again, his primary responsibility is to promote and
protect the health of his patient. He has no responsibility to respect
the wishes—or presumed wishes—of the patient himself to forgo that
which is genuinely called for medically: procedures he knows, in his
position as "first mate" to health, are called for.

Sometimes a remedy a doctor believes makes sense medically
runs into impediments of a financial or even legal nature. In such
situations, there is often a bit of leeway, so that a well-intentioned
doctor can, without lying, issue a description of a patient's situation
such as makes the remedy available. But he may in the end have to
throw up his hands and acknowledge that he can do nothing. Such
a situation may or may not be an unjust one. Insurance companies
and governmental entities are bound by particular precepts of their
own—precepts presumably in accordance with the more general precepts of justice—and following these precepts may very well entail
that someone is deprived of a remedy that is called for medically. It
can be a governmental entity's proper role to decide where and how
health resources are to be allocated: which districts or which age
groups shall have access to a limited number of dialysis machines, for
instance.[6] When resources are limited, very likely someone will not
be receiving care that is called for medically.

A duly appointed governmental entity acts within its proper competency when making such allocations. Of course, it must ensure that
they are made in accordance with justice. No government, however,
can ever legitimately impose a practice upon medicine that involves

6. Recall what we heard Aristotle (seconded by Thomas) saying above: "it is the
concern of the householder and *the ruler* to think about health."

direct killing—or any other immoral practice or means, such as artificial contraception or sterilization. Government's proper task in this regard is the allocation of resources, not the prescribing of medical procedures (which is the proper responsibility of medicine)—and *certainly* not the prescribing of procedures that violate the central precept of medicine to "do no harm to the patient" (see above, chapter 2).

At this point we have before us the moral principles required in order to address the (in certain circles) controversial issue of the administration of nutrition and hydration to incapacitated patients. In March of 2004, in an address to the participants of a Roman academic conference on life-sustaining treatments and the so-called "vegetative state," Pope John Paul II made the following remark:

> I should like particularly to underline how the administration of water and food, even when provided by artificial means, always represents a natural means of preserving life, not a medical act. Its use, furthermore, should be considered, in principle, ordinary and proportionate, and as such morally obligatory, insofar as and until it is seen to have attained its proper finality, which in the present case consists in providing nourishment to the patient and alleviation of his suffering.[7]

This statement was met with resistance by some sectors of the Catholic academic community and was even dismissed as nonmagisterial: it was interpreted by some as a statement put into the hands of an aging and confused pontiff by the organizers of the conference. But, in

---

7. John Paul II also notes that "the term 'permanent vegetative state' has been coined to indicate the condition of those patients whose 'vegetative state' continues for over a year. Actually, there is no different diagnosis that corresponds to such a definition, but only a conventional prognostic judgment, relative to the fact that the recovery of patients, statistically speaking, is ever more difficult as the condition of vegetative state is prolonged in time." The CDF's commentary on its own 2007 document quotes this latter remark and adds (in a note): "Terminology concerning the different phases and forms of the 'vegetative state' continues to be discussed, but this is not important for the moral judgment involved."

August of 2007, the Congregation for the Doctrine of the Faith (the CDF) issued an official response to "certain questions of the United States Conference of Catholic Bishops concerning artificial nutrition and hydration" that basically repeated what John Paul II had said in 2004, making even more clear that the reason for providing nutrition and hydration is not only to avoid patients' suffering but also to prevent "death by starvation and dehydration." Although the response of the CDF speaks of patients in a permanent vegetative state, the commentary that accompanied the response makes it apparent that the principle set out in the response applies in other situations, as well.

A couple of things are especially worthy of notice, given the ideas set out so far in the present chapter. First of all, John Paul II says in the 2004 address that the administration of nutrition and hydration, even when done by artificial means, is "not a medical act." On the other hand, he also notes that it is required only "insofar as and until it is seen to have attained its proper finality." The CDF's commentary on its 2007 document clarifies this latter point by acknowledging (1) that, in "very remote places or in situations of extreme poverty," *artificial* administration may not be obligatory (because impossible), (2) that, in any economic context, "due to emerging complications, a patient may be unable to assimilate food and liquids, so that their provision becomes altogether useless," and (3) that "in some rare cases, artificial nourishment and hydration may be excessively burdensome for the patient or may cause significant physical discomfort, for example resulting from complications in the use of the means employed." What the inclusion of these exceptions demonstrates is that, while the obligation to administer nutrition and hydration may not be a positive precept of *medicine,* it is a positive precept—that is, a positive precept of ethics in the more general sense, and so (as usual) the omission of that for which it is calls is culpable only so long as the positive precept is operative. To use the language introduced above, the obligation to provide nutrition and hydration is applicable "always but not at every moment."

Since the precept calling for the administration of nutrition and hydration is a precept of ethics itself rather than just of medicine, even though (as a positive precept) it does not apply "always and at every moment," it does apply always and at *practically* every moment, for it is binding upon human beings *qua* human beings (or, perhaps, *qua* social beings). The exceptions enter into most modern cultural contexts only in the last hours of a person's life. Thus, it is obligatory to provide nutrition and hydration, even by artificial means, to persons in a vegetative state, since such persons, by virtue of being in such a state, are not in imminent danger of dying (unless, of course, they are deprived of nutrition and hydration—which would be to kill them by way of an omission). It is obligatory to provide nutrition and hydration, not necessarily but possibly by artificial means, also to persons not in such a state, since to do otherwise would be to kill them.

It is generally recognized that toward the end of life—when this end is brought on by various diseases or simply by old age—the human body itself begins to reject nutrition (and less frequently hydration). Hospice workers sometimes speak of the body's "shutting down." In such situations, the positive obligation to provide nutrition (and possibly hydration) is no longer operative, for those means can no longer attain their "proper finality, which is the hydration and nourishment of the patient," as the CDF's 2007 response expresses the crucial point of John Paul II's 2004 address. Of course, before omitting to administer food or hydration, hospital staff, hospice workers, and/or family must know with moral certainty that the patient's body is indeed "shutting down."

Both of these documents speak of the administration of nutrition and hydration as not only "ordinary," but also "proportionate." This proportion (or suitableness) has nothing immediately or necessarily to do with the financial or human resources to be allotted to care of the patient—the CDF's commentary states, in fact, that the required means are "within the capacity of an average health-care system"—but with the means' suitability for accomplishing the relevant purpose, "which is to keep the patient from dying of starvation and dehydration." When accomplishing this purpose is not a possibility, a family member or other person who decides not to administer nutrition and hydration is recognizing that the captain of the ship—nature, as manifest in the person's health—can no longer be helped. The omission is not an immoral omission.

Most life-and-death decisions turn on the efficacy of particular medical procedures in defeating or controlling disease and on the means—both financial and human—at the disposal of the patient or his closest relatives for the continuation of care. Although it always makes sense for someone to prefer to live longer (for death is not a positive thing, but a consequence rather of original sin [ST 1-2.85.5]), it can also be right for someone to decide not to burden his family or himself by initiating a particular procedure. Take the example of a man, eighty years old, who has cancer of the lungs and who has also undergone chemotherapy over a period of two or three years, but who has been told that the cancer has reappeared. He knows what chemotherapy is like and that undergoing a new round of treatments will be extremely difficult physically and will entail intensive medical attention and considerable expense. He has the insurance coverage that would cover the expense, but wonders "whether it is worth it." He lost his wife a few years ago, and with her departed his only real reason for living. He cannot honestly say to himself that he is unafraid of death, but he knows that death is not far off in any case ... and he believes that there is life after death for those who have not separated themselves from Christ. If he decides not to undergo the proposed chemotherapy, would he be killing himself? "For, after all," as he might reason to himself, "at certain moments I really *want* to die. If I do that which causes this to happen—refusing further treatment—am I not killing myself?"

John Paul II's discourse and the CDF's response to the American bishops are helpful here. As we have seen, since the precept "administer nutrition and hydration" is a positive precept (a very general positive precept), it does allow for cases in which an omission is ethically permissible. Both John Paul II's discourse and the CDF's response also say that a permissible omission is one that does not constitute *killing* the patient by dehydration or starvation. When the omission is ethically acceptable, something else is responsible for the death: the disease itself. In the case of the eighty-year-old cancer patient who forgoes further chemotherapy, the issue is not the administration or withdrawal of nutrition and hydration; operative rather is the same principle that sometimes allows one not to administer nutrition and hydration—that is, the principle governing positive precepts. The man can forgo the chemotherapy; in this case, it is clear that what kills him is the cancer and not the forgoing of the treatment.

This is not to say that, in any situation in which a disease might be allowed to run its course and to kill, it is ethical to omit treatment. Take the case of a young woman who omits treatments for curable cancer because she has broken up with her boyfriend and wants to die. Even discounting possible clouding of her judgment due to depression, on the face of it this case is quite different from that of the eighty-year-old with terminal cancer. The older man has in *any* case not long to live: he will never recover full bodily integrity; the gradual disintegration of his body caused by the cancer (and old age) can only be slowed down, not arrested. If the young woman continues with her chemotherapy, she will quite likely regain her health and maintain bodily integrity for years to come. If she chooses to discontinue the chemotherapy, even though the cancer would be the cause of death, she would be killing herself—"by means of the cancer," so to speak. Her omission would fall within the obligatory scope of the positive precept that might be formulated as "Adopt healthy practices in order to ensure bodily integrity."

To go back to the image of the ship, for the young woman to decline to follow the regimen of chemotherapy would be like the first mate's failing to follow the commands of the captain (health). It is presumed that the captain understands both medical situations: he would not, therefore, order the first mate (medicine) to prolong the life of the eighty-year-old cancer patient, but he would quite reasonably order the first mate to prolong the life of the young woman. To say that the captain would not issue the order in the case of the eighty-year-old just means that the positive precept—"Adopt healthy practices in order to ensure bodily integrity"—is not in effect, for the desired bodily integrity cannot be maintained. To say that the captain would issue the order in the case of the young woman is to say that she can and ought to follow the regimen of chemotherapy—for otherwise she would be killing herself. There is no fixed rule for determining when a case is more like that of the eighty-year-old than that of the young woman. Those who are faced with such decisions must be prudent—prudent, that is, in the classical sense: they must possess and apply good judgment.

This way of approaching such matters provides us with an answer to a possible objection to the John Paul II–CDF requirement that nutrition and hydration be administered (except in certain extreme situations). The objection might be expressed in the following manner: "The church says that nutrition and hydration are not extraordinary means (and, therefore, almost never to be withheld); she regards, however, a respirator as extraordinary means (and, therefore, in many cases, capable of being withheld morally). But the use of a respirator is not very different from the administration of nutrition and hydration, for food and water are not very different from air: we need them all in order to live. The church is, therefore, inconsistent: the administration of nutrition and hydration, especially by artificial means, ought to be considered extraordinary medical means."

A reasonable response to this objection would begin by admitting that, in a certain sense, the precept regarding the use of a respirator is not radically different from that regarding the artificial administration of nutrition and hydration: in either case, we are dealing with a positive precept, and positive precepts do not apply always and at every moment. When the church's magisterium employs terms such as "ordinary means," "medical means," and "extraordinary means," it is not giving a philosophical account of such actions and situations; it is simply attaching standard labels to typical cases. When the cases of moral withholding are numerous, the label "extraordinary means" is used; when they are few, the label "ordinary means" (or "nonmedical means") is used. But both ways of speaking presuppose a positive precept that does not apply always and at every moment.

There is, however, a good philosophical reason for this differentiated use of labels. Although nutrition, hydration, and air are all things that go into the human body and are necessary for its continued existence as a unified living whole, nutrition and hydration get into the body in a way different from the way air does. Air is always—or, at least, usually—*there:* a person need not go out in order to acquire it or have it brought to him. A person does have to do something in order to acquire nutrition and hydration, or they have to be brought to him.

This is not just a cultural difference between two practices, but has a direct bearing upon the nature of the action involved when one or the other does not arrive. Feeding, eating, etc., involve human (voluntary) acts; breathing usually does not: in general, respiration is involuntary. This makes culpable omission more possible in the former case, less possible in the latter. In failing to provide nutrition and hydration, there is less—indeed, almost no—scope to claim, "It was an independently operating pathology that took his life." But that is usually an accurate description of what happens when someone dies of respiratory problems. In other words, even when removing a respirator is immoral, it does not involve a positive human act *per se* directed at the taking of life. If one fails to bring nutrition and hydration to an incapacitated person (who is capable of assimilating the same), one is starving him or causing him to die of thirst. If one unplugs a respirator, one is not *suffocating* the person on it. What eventually kills the patient is whatever pathology it was that prevented him from breathing on his own. It may indeed be the case that one is killing the person by depriving him of the means that were allowing him to breathe (and that would be murder); but, even still, one is not impeding him from doing something (breathing) that he could—and would—have otherwise done on his own.

This distinction is clearly morally relevant. It explains why it is easier for someone to say truthfully "I did not kill the other person, but the pathology impeding respiration did so." In other words, and to use the traditional label, the distinction helps to explain why respirators are typically considered extraordinary means. This does not mean that a person not helping oxygen to arrive where it should can always claim not to have killed the other person. Imagine an employee well-trained in the emergency procedures to be used when individuals are choking, including the Heimlich maneuver. He opens the door to the office of his boss—whom he hates—just as the latter is choking on a piece of chicken; instead of performing the Heimlich maneuver, he gently closes the office door and walks away. In this case, the employee has killed his boss by means of his omission. Similarly, a doctor who knows that continued use of a respirator will allow a patient to be breathing on his own in a week's time, but disconnects it because he thinks the patient's life not worth living, kills that patient. He kills the patient by means of his allowing the pathology to work its effect unimpeded when he ought not to have done so—i.e., when the positive precept governing his action required that he not omit the respirator.

This difference between withholding nutrition and hydration and unplugging a respirator is what allows John Paul II and the CDF to say that nutrition and hydration are not extraordinary means. As we have seen, however, the magisterium of the church acknowledges that in certain circumstances nutrition and hydration do indeed become extraordinary means. In such circumstances, withholding them is like turning off a respirator in appropriate circumstances and allowing an underlying pathology to have its inevitable effect. But, in almost all circumstances, withholding nutrition and hydration is not like that, but constitutes killing by starvation and/or dehydration. The number of cases in which the omission falls within the obligatory scope of the positive precept ("feed and give drink to the hungry and thirsty") is much larger than with the use of respirators; or, conversely, the obligatory scope of the positive precept "keep the respiratory pathways clear and operative" is narrower, although not so narrow as to permit a doctor to disconnect a respirator for reasons other than its futility.

BIBLIOGRAPHICAL MATTERS

In this book, *ST* stands for Thomas Aquinas's *Summa theologiae*. The first bit of the reference that follows the *ST* stands for a part of the *Summa*: 1 = the first part; 1-2 = the first part of the second part; 2-2 = the second part of the second part; 3 = the third part. The next bit stands for the pertinent question or questions; the bit that follows stands for the article within a question. Sometimes after an article number, one finds a "c," referring to the *corpus* (or main argument of the article), or the Latin word "a" ("in response to") with a numeral, referring to one of Aquinas's responses to one of the objections with which the relevant article begins. Thus, "*ST* 2-2. 64.7.ad 2" refers to the second part of the second part of the *Summa*, the sixty-fourth question, the seventh article, the response to the second objection; "*ST* 1-2.94.2c" refers to the first part of the second part of the *Summa*, the ninety-fourth question, the second article, the *corpus*.

The best complete English translation of the *Summa theologiae* is *Thomas Aquinas, Summa Theologica*, translated by the Fathers of the English Dominican Province (London: Burns, Oates and Washbourne, 1920); this was reissued by the Benziger Brothers in 1948 and reprinted many times since. It is currently published by Christian Classics, which also makes the translation available online and as a downloadable PDF file.

The standard English translation of the works of Aristotle is *The Complete Works of Aristotle: The Revised Oxford Translation* (Princeton, N.J.: Princeton University Press, 1984), edited by Jonathan Barnes. A good translation of just the *Nicomachean Ethics* is Terence Irwin's *Aristotle: Nichomachean Ethics* (Indianapolis, Ind., and Cambridge: Hackett

Publishing, 1985). Most translations of Aristotle's works include marginal numbers, called "Bekker numbers," corresponding to individual lines of the Greek text. In the case of the *Nicomachean Ethics*, these more precise indicators are often crucial, since there are in use two systems of dividing that work's books into chapters. I use the chapter divisions of Barnes's *Revised Oxford Translation*. A standard reference would be "*EN* iii.1.1111a3–21," where *EN* = *Nicomachean Ethics*, iii = book 3, 1 = chapter 1, and 1111a3–21 indicates the Bekker line numbers. The now superseded edition of Aristotle's works by Immanuel Bekker had two columns of Greek per page: the letter "a" in "1111a3–21" refers to the first column; were the letter not "a," but "b," the reference would be to the second column (of page 1111, lines 3 to 21).

Most of the church documents mentioned in this book (including the *Catechism of the Catholic Church*), are available on the Holy See's website. Occasionally I refer to the collections of official documents: the *Acta Sanctae Sedis* and the later *Acta Apostolicae Sedis*. The standard abbreviation for the former is "ASS," for the latter "AAS."

Chapter 1: Is Moral Teaching the Church's?

Thomas's "Treatise on Law," mentioned in this chapter, is found at *ST* 1-2.90–108. St. Augustine's *De libero arbitrio* (*On Free Choice* or *On Free Choice of the Will*), also mentioned, is translated by Robert P. Russell and included in *St. Augustine: The Teacher; The Free Choice of the Will; Grace and Free Will*, The Fathers of the Church: A New Translation (Washington, D.C.: The Catholic University of America Press, 1968), 59:63–241. The passage I cite in chapter 1 is book 1, chapters 5 and 6.

Useful church documents include two of the constitutions promulgated by the Second Vatican Council: *Lumen gentium* ["Dogmatic Constitution on the Church"] and *Gaudium et spes* ["Pastoral Constitution on the Church in the Modern World"]. Especially pertinent to the themes of this chapter are §§30–38 of *Lumen gentium*, regarding the role of the laity, and §§63–82 of *Gaudium et spes*, regarding public life.

See also the *Catechism of the Catholic Church*, part 3, section 1, chapter 2, article 2, §§1897–1904; part 3, section 1, chapter 3, article 1 (§§1950–86) and article 3 (§§2030–51); and part 3, section 2, chapter 2, article 5 (§§2258–2330); see also the *Compendium of the Catechism of the Catholic*

Church (Washington, D.C.: United States Conference of Catholic Bishops, 2005), part 3, section w1, chapter 2, §§405–6; part 3, section 1, chapter 3, §§415–21 and 429–33; and part 3, section 2, chapter 2 (§§466–86).

See also the relevant sections in the *Compendium of the Social Doctrine of the Church,* by the Pontifical Council for Justice and Peace (Rome: Libreria Editrice Vaticana, 2005).

John Paul II published two major encyclicals on ethical questions: *Veritatis splendor* and *Evangelium vitae;* see especially *Veritatis splendor,* chapter 2 (§§28–83) and *Evangelium vitae,* chapter 3 (§§52–77).

Pertinent also are a number of documents published by the Congregation for the Doctrine of the Faith, including: "Doctrinal Note on Some Questions Regarding the Participation of Catholics in Political Life" (July 2003); "Some Considerations Concerning the Response to Legislative Proposals on the Non-discrimination of Homosexual Persons" (July 1992); and "Declaration on Procured Abortion" (November 1974).

A useful essay for understanding the relationships among natural, eternal, and divine law is G. E. M. Anscombe's "Authority in Morals" in her *Collected Philosophical Papers,* vol. 3, *Ethics, Religion and Politics* (Minneapolis, Minn.: University of Minnesota Press, 1981), 43–50.

Chapter 2: The Intelligibility of Human Action

The basic ideas presented in this chapter are taken (also by Thomas) from chapter 1 of book 3 of the *Nicomachean Ethics,* i.e., from *EN* iii.1.1109b30–111b3. For an exposition of the early chapters of *EN* iii, see Michael Pakaluk's *Aristotle's* Nicomachean Ethics: *An Introduction* (Cambridge: Cambridge University Press, 2005), chap. 4. Cicero's list of the circumstances of human action is found in an early work of his called *De inventione* (at 1.26).

Thomas's most accessible treatment of the sources of morality is at *ST* 1-2.6–21; article 18 is particularly important. For an exposition of his theory of human action, see Ralph McInerny's *Aquinas on Human Action: A Theory of Practice* (Washington, D.C.: The Catholic University of America Press, 1992); see also Stephen Brock's *Action and Conduct: Thomas Aquinas and the Theory of Action* (Edinburgh: T. and T. Clark, 1998); Archbishop Eric D'Arcy's *Human Acts: An Essay in Their Moral Evaluation* (Oxford: Clarendon Press, 1963); Joseph Pilsner's *The Specifi-*

cation of Human Actions in St. Thomas Aquinas (Oxford: Oxford University Press, 2006); and Elizabeth Anscombe's *Intention* (Oxford: Blackwell, 1957).

John Paul II discusses the sources of morality at *Veritatis splendor*, §74, the number in which he speaks of placing oneself "in the perspective of the acting person." Especially pertinent to the material of this chapter are §§71–83 of that encyclical.

Conscience is treated in the *Catechism of the Catholic Church* in §§1776–1802 (part 3, section 1, chapter 1, article 6). *Veritatis splendor* also has a section on "Conscience and Truth" (§§54–64). In Thomas, the key articles are *ST* 1-2.19.5 and 6. See also the works mentioned below in connection with chapter 6 (which is about conscience).

An account of the controversy, eventually resolved, regarding the morality of the removal of a cancerous gravid (pregnant) uterus as opposed to other procedures (such as craniotomy) in which the fetus is killed directly is given in Fr. John Connery's *Abortion: The Development of the Roman Catholic Perspective* (Chicago: Loyola University Press, 1977), chap. 12–15. On May 31, 1884, the predecessor of the Congregation for the Doctrine of the Faith declared that it was not safe to teach that craniotomy is not immoral [ASS 17:556]; but in 1930, while declaring that direct killing of a fetus in order to save the mother is immoral, Pius XI cited the 1884 document (see the encyclical letter *Casti conubii* §64). Pius XI's declaration concerns not merely *teaching* regarding such killing; it concerns rather the killing itself. A similar thing can be said of a decree issued by the same congregation on July 24, 1895—that is, that the decree did not limit itself to saying only that such teaching was unsafe [ASS 28:383–84].

On the objects of physical movements (including human actions), see Aristotle's *Physics* iii.1–3 and v.1–6; see also Stephen Brock's *Action and Conduct: Thomas Aquinas and the Theory of Action* (Edinburgh: T. and T. Clark, 1998), chap. 1–3.

On the Hippocratic Oath, see Leon R. Kass, *Toward a More Natural Science: Biology and Human Affairs* (New York: Free Press, 1985), chap. 9.

Chapter 3: Moral Absolutes, Sexual Morality, Reproductive Ethics

In *Nicomachean Ethics* ii.6.1107a8–27, Aristotle recognizes that certain types of acts are always wrong; he mentions adultery, stealing, and murder. On the interpretation of this passage, see John Finnis's *Moral Absolutes: Tradition, Revision and Truth* (Washington, D.C.: The Catholic University of America Press, 1991), chap. 2. In Thomas, see especially *ST* 1-2.18.1 and 5. At *EN* iv.7.1127a28–30, Aristotle says that "falsehood is *per se* foul and reprehensible; the truth, noble and praiseworthy."

The *Catechism of the Catholic Church* speaks about lying in §§2482–87 (part 3, section 2, chapter 2, article 8). Note, however, that the *editio typica,* published in 1997, made some alterations to the original, provisional version of the *Catechism.* In particular, the second sentence in the original §2483 read, "To lie is to speak or act against the truth in order to lead into error someone who has the right to know the truth." In current English translation of the *editio typica,* that sentence now reads, "To lie is to speak or act against the truth in order to lead someone into error." The *Catechism* (§2482) cites St. Augustine's *De mendacio* (*About Lying*); Augustine also wrote another treatise entitled *Contra mendacium* (*Against Lying*). Both are included in volume 16 of The Fathers of the Church series, published by the Catholic University Press of America.

A translation of the Congregation for the Doctrine of the Faith's decree "Regarding Impotence That Invalidates Marriage" can be found in the *National Catholic Bioethics Quarterly* 6 (2006): 753–54. The translation is appended to an article by Fr. Urbano Navarrete discussing the decree's level of authority (736–52 of the same number of the *National Catholic Bioethics Quarterly*).

There are many English translations of *Humanae vitae* in circulation; the best, in my opinion, is the version translated by John Finnis: *Encyclical Letter* Humanae Vitae *of the Supreme Pontiff Pope Paul VI* (London: The Incorporated Catholic Truth Society, 2008). Vatican II's *Gaudium et spes* discusses marriage and the family in §§47–52; see also *Catholic Sexual Ethics: A Summary, Explanation, and Defense,* by Ronald Lawler, Joseph M. Boyle, and William E. May (Huntington, Ind.: Our Sunday Visitor, 1998).

The Church's bioethical teaching is stated most succinctly in *Donum vitae* (*The Gift of Life*) and *Dignitas personae* (*Dignity of the Person*), both published by the Congregation for the Doctrine of the Faith. Other ecclesial documents relevant to the argument of chapter 3 are quoted there in the footnotes; see also William E. May's *Catholic Bioethics and the Gift of Human Life* (Huntington, Ind.: Our Sunday Visitor, 2000).

Bits of this chapter are taken from my essay "'In This Regard, the Teaching of the Magisterium Is Already Explicit': On *Dignitas Personae* §12," in *Fertility and Gender: Issues in Reproductive and Sexual Ethics*, edited by Helen Watt (Oxford: Anscombe Bioethics Centre, 2011), 184–200.

Chapter 4: The Ethics of Killing

On Aristotle's methodology in ethics, see Michael Pakaluk's *Aristotle's Nicomachean Ethics: An Introduction,* 25–37.

The *Catechism of the Catholic Church* discusses the ethics of killing in part 3, section 2, chapter 2, article 5 (§§2258–2330); often cited (also by the *Catechism*: §§2263–64) with respect to the ethics of killing is Thomas's *ST* 2-2.64.7.

On war and just war, see Cicero, *De officiis* (*On Duties*), i.34–40; see also Augustine, *Civitas Dei* (*City of God*), xv.5, xix.7; Augustine, *De libero arbitrio* (*On Free Choice* or *On Free Choice of the Will*), i.5, and Augustine, *Contra Faustum* (*Against Faustus*), xxii.75; see Thomas Aquinas, *ST* 2-2.40.1; see also the *Catechism of the Catholic Church,* part 3, section 2, chapter 2, article 5, §§2302–17; and John C. Ford, "The Morality of Obliteration Bombing," *Theological Studies* 5 (1944): 261–309; and Ford, "The Hydrogen Bombing of Cities," *Theology Digest* 18 (1957): 6–9.

Chapter 5: Cooperation in Evil

As mentioned in this chapter, John Paul II's *Evangelium vitae* §73 is central to the controversy about voting for "imperfect legislation." A book whose main argument has to do with imperfect legislation and *Evangelium vitae* §73 is Colin Harte's *Changing Unjust Laws Justly: Pro-Life Solidarity with "The Last and Least"* (Washington, D.C.: The Catholic University of America Press, 2005). See also the debate between Harte and John Finnis in *Cooperation, Complicity and Conscience: Problems in Law and Public Policy,* edited by Helen Watt (London: Linacre Centre, 2005).

On cooperation, see *Evangelium vitae* §74; in the *Catechism of the Catholic Church,* see part 3, section 1, chapter 1, article 8, §1868 and part 3, section 2, chapter 2, article 5, §2272 and §2291. Many of the ideas in Elizabeth Anscombe's *Intention* (Oxford: Blackwell, 1957) are pertinent to the issue of cooperation. Thomas discusses intention at *ST* 1-2.12.

Mentioned in this chapter are two documents published by the Congregation for the Doctrine of the Faith: "Some Considerations Concerning the Response to Legislative Proposals on the Non-discrimination of Homosexual Persons" (July 1992) and "Considerations Regarding Proposals to Give Legal Recognition to Unions Between Homosexual Persons" (July 2003).

For Thomas's position on "allowable vices," see *ST* 1-2.96.2; see also Robert P. George's *Making Men Moral: Civil Liberties and Public Morality* (Oxford: Clarendon Press, 1993), especially 21–47; see also John Finnis, *Aquinas: Moral, Political and Legal Theory* (Oxford: Oxford University Press, 1998), especially 2222–28. On the role of judges, see Thomas Aquinas, *ST* 2-2.67 and 64.6; see also Augustine's *City of God* 19.6.

On equity, see *ST* 1-2.96.6 and 2-2.120. In Aristotle, see *EN* v.10.1137a31–1138a3 and *Rhetoric* i.13, in particular, 1374a25–b23.

Chapter 6: *The Supremacy of Conscience*

As mentioned above, in chapter 2's bibliographic notes, the *Catechism of the Catholic Church* considers conscience in §§1776–1802 (part 3, section 1, chapter 1, article 6); a section of *Veritatis splendor* is also devoted to "Conscience and Truth" (§§54–64). In the documents of Vatican II, see *Gaudium et spes* §16, *Unitatis redintegratio* (especially §3), and *Dignitatis humanae.*

Thomas Aquinas discusses *synderesis* and *conscientia* in his commentary on Peter Lombard's *Sentences* (book 2, distinction 24, questions 2 and 3; distinction 39, question 3); see *Scriptum super Libros Sententiarum Magistri Petri Lombardi Episcopi Parisiensis,* edited by Pierre Mandonnet and Maria Fabianus Moos (Paris: Lethielleux, 1929–1947); for book 2, see vol. 2, edited by Mandonnet (1929). Unfortunately, no translation of this commentary is available in English. He discusses *synderesis* and *conscientia* also in the *Disputed Questions on Truth,* abbreviated in the footnotes to this chapter as *QD de ver.,* questions 16 and 17, respectively. An English translation of this work was done by Robert Mulligan, SJ, and is available as *Truth: St. Thomas Aquinas* (Indianapolis, Ind.: Hackett Publishing, 1994); originally published in Chicago by H. Regnery, 1952–1954). Thomas discusses *synderesis* in *ST* 1.79.12–13 and in *ST* 1-2.94.1; in *ST* 1-2.19.5 and 6, he discusses *conscientia* and its relation to reason.

In the main text of chapter 6, I mention the important passage in the first chapter of the third book of Aristotle's *Nicomachean Ethics*, 1110b32–33. There is another important passage in book 7, chapter 9 (1151a35–b4), the importance of which becomes apparent in Thomas's commentary on the passage; *Commentary on the Nicomachean Ethics*, translated by C. I. Litzinger, foreword by Ralph McInerny (Notre Dame, Ind.: Dumb Ox Books, 1993; originally published in Chicago by H. Regnery, 1964), §1483. At *Eudemian Ethics* ii.9.1225b14–16, Aristotle mentions one's responsibility to know what is permitted and forbidden.

Two useful, more contemporary books would be Eric D'Arcy's *Conscience and Its Right to Freedom* (New York: Sheed and Ward, 1961) and the volume edited by John Haas, *Crisis of Conscience* (New York: Crossroad, 1996). The latter contains an essay on conscience ("Conscience and Truth") by then Cardinal Joseph Ratzinger. Also very useful in the same volume is Ralph McInerny's "Conscience and the Object of the Moral Act." See also McInerny's "Prudence and Conscience," *The Thomist* 38 (1974): 291–305. G. E. M. Anscombe's "On Being in Good Faith" is also well worth reading; see *Faith in a Hard Ground: Essays on Religion, Philosophy, and Ethics by G. E. M. Anscombe,* edited by Mary Geach and Luke Gormally (Exeter, U.K., and Charlottesville, Va.: Imprint Academic, 2008), 101–12.

John Henry Newman is often cited with respect to conscience (including at *Catechism of the Catholic Church* §1778); see his "A Letter Addressed to His Grace the Duke of Norfolk on Occasion of Mr. Gladstone's Recent Expostulation," in *Certain Difficulties Felt by Anglicans in Catholic Teaching Considered* (London: Burns and Oates, 1879), 2:171–378; see also John Finnis's "Conscience in the *Letter to the Duke of Norfolk,*" in *Newman After a Hundred Years,* edited by Ian Ker and Alan G. Hill (Oxford: Clarendon, 1990), 401–18.

Chapter 7: Life-and-Death Decisions

Thomas Aquinas's position on omissions is set out in *ST* 1-2.6.3; see also *ST* 1-2.71.5.

In *Veritatis splendor* §§13–15 and (especially) §52, John Paul II recognizes the distinction between positive and negative precepts. Thomas discusses the distinction in *ST* 1-2.71.5 ad 2, *Sent.* 2.22.2.1 ad 4 and 2.35.1.3 ad 3 and *De malo* 2.1 ad 11 (a). His position comes out of a brief remark in Aristotle's *Nicomachean Ethics*, at iii.5.1113b11–21.

Relevant church documents include John Paul II's address "To the Participants in the 'International Congress on Life-sustaining Treatments and Vegetative State: Scientific Advances and Ethical Dilemmas'" (March 20, 2004) and the Congregation for the Doctrine of the Faith's "Responses to Certain Questions of the United States Conference of Catholic Bishops Concerning Artificial Nutrition and Hydration" (August 2007), plus the commentary on the same. The latter demonstrates in a well-documented manner that John Paul II's remarks in March of 2004 were consistent and consonant with church teaching by popes and Roman dicasteries since the pontificate of Pius XII; it serves, therefore, as a good review of the teaching's history.

On the administration of nutrition and hydration to dying patients, see Erik J. Meidl, "A Case Studies Approach to Assisted Nutrition and Hydration," *National Catholic Bioethics Quarterly* 6 (2006): 319–36; see also L. John Hoffer, "Tube Feeding in Advanced Dementia: The Metabolic Perspective," *BMJ: British Medical Journal* 333, no. 7580 (2006): 1214–15. Useful on the lack of evidence for the thesis that persons in persistent vegetative states do not think is Donald E. Henke, "Consciousness, Terri Schiavo, and the Persistent Vegetative State," *National Catholic Bioethics Quarterly* 8 (2008): 69–85.

Very useful on all life-and-death issues is William E. May's *Catholic Bioethics and the Gift of Human Life* (Huntington, Ind.: Our Sunday Visitor, 2000), chap. 7.

GENERAL INDEX

INDEX OF PASSAGES CITED FROM AQUINAS
AND FROM ARISTOTLE

Aquinas, St. Thomas

Aristotle

ALSO FROM THE IPS PRESS

The John Henry Cardinal Newman Lectures
EDITED BY CRAIG STEVEN TITUS

1. *The Person and the Polis: Faith and Values within the Secular State* (2007)

2. *On Wings of Faith and Reason: The Christian Difference in Culture and Science* (2008)

3. *Christianity and the West: Interaction and Impact in Art and Culture* (2009)

4. *The Psychology of Character and Virtue* (2009)

5. *Philosophical Psychology* (2009)

Monograph Series

1. Fergus Kerr, *"Work on Oneself": Wittgenstein's Philosophical Psychology* (2008)

2. Kenneth L. Schmitz, *Person and Psyche* (2009)